An integrated course for communicative success

Wanna Talk

1

PAGODA Books

INTRODUCTION

Wanna Talk 1 is the first book in the **Wanna Talk** series, a three-level course specially designed for beginner or false beginner level adult students who are studying English as a foreign language. It gives students more opportunities than other books of its kind to learn and practice English. The course combines topics, functions and grammar in practical and authentic ways. The primary goal of the course is to help students communicate appropriately according to the situation, purpose and roles of the participants. Students will learn the four main skills of listening, speaking, reading and writing in addition to vocabulary and pronunciation.

What each unit contains...

Start and Dialogue

The **Start** section introduces the unit's frequently used vocabulary in diverse ways. The **Dialogue** section allows students to preview the unit's principal grammar points and topic. It also creates interest in the unit.

Grammar

The **Grammar** section of each unit is clearly presented, and the most important points are exemplified with practical sample sentences.

Speak

There are usually three **Speak** sections in a unit. The length and difficulty increases from **Speak 1** to **Speak 3**. Apart from the typical drill activities, students can practice more functional and authentic English conversations through the **Speak** sections.

Activity

One of the strongest points of this book is that there are various kinds of activities which incorporate reading and writing as well as speaking. Language is learned best when skills are learned holistically. Students can practice the target grammar points and important expressions collaboratively or on their own.

Listen and Pronunciation

The **Listen** section helps students develop a wide variety of listening skills. Also, the **Pronunciation** section provides students with different types of activities dealing with problems that they have regarding pronunciation in English.

CONTENTS

- Introduction — 2
- Contents — 3
- Scope and Sequence — 4

- **UNIT 01** Nice to meet you — 8
- **UNIT 02** Who is she? — 14
- **UNIT 03** There is a cell phone on the table — 20
- **UNIT 04** That's mine! — 26
- **UNIT 05** What are you doing? — 32
- **UNIT 06** Does he go to work early? — 38
- **UNIT 07** What does she do? — 44
- **UNIT 08** Can you dance well? — 50
- **UNIT 09** Where was he last night? — 56
- **UNIT 10** What did you do yesterday? — 62
- **UNIT 11** How many apples do you need? — 68
- **UNIT 12** I'd like to go rollerblading — 74
- **UNIT 13** He's tall and funny — 80
- **UNIT 14** I go jogging every day — 86
- **UNIT 15** What are you going to do tonight? — 92
- **UNIT 16** Could you tell me how to get there? — 98

- Grammar Exercises — 104
- Listening Script — 120
- Answer Key for Pronunciation — 124
- Answer Key for Grammar Exercises — 127

SCOPE AND SEQUENCE

Unit	Topics	Grammar
01 Nice to meet you	Greeting and introduction	**Be verb 1:** affirmative and negative statements; Yes/No questions and short answers
02 Who is she?	3rd person's personal information; special occasions	**Be verb 2:** information questions and affirmative answers
03 There is a cell phone on the table	Household items; personal belongings; office supplies	Regular and irregular plural nouns; prepositions of place
04 That's mine!	Personal belongings; family; shopping	Subject/possessive pronouns; possessive adjectives, whose
05 What are you doing?	Daily activities; time	Present progressive
06 Does he go to work early?	Daily routines; free time activities	**Simple present 1:** Yes/No questions; 3rd person singular
07 What does she do?	Occupations; weekend activities	**Simple present 2:** Wh- questions and affirmative answers
08 Can you dance well?	Abilities; requests	*Can* for ability and wh- questions; *can* for request

Speaking	Reading Writing	Listening Pronunciation
• Talking about names and nationalities • Identifying people	• Writing about personal information after interviewing	• Listening for telephone numbers • Stress of words for country and nationality
• Talking about 3rd person's personal information and dates of special occasions	• Writing about celebrities' personal information	• Listening to information questions • Pronunciation of -teen and -ty; ordinal numbers
• Talking about numbers and locations of household items or office supplies	• Writing about the locations of things • Writing about dream houses	• Listening to find the locations of household items • Pronunciation of plural nouns ending sound
• Talking about personal belongings	• Writing about the relationships in a family	• Listening for correct subject and possessive pronouns • Pronunciation of singular and plural nouns
• Talking about what people are doing at present	• Writing about what other people are doing • Reading about text messages	• Listening to find out what other people are doing • Intonation of yes/no questions and wh-questions
• Talking about daily routines and free time activities	• Reading about a person's daily schedule	• Listening to people talk about their lives • Pronunciation of 3rd person singular ending sounds
• Talking about people's occupations and daily schedules	• Writing about people's occupations	• Listening to people's daily or weekend schedules • Linking *wh-* and *do*
• Talking about abilities and requests	• Reading advertisements	• Listen to what people can do • Identifying *can* or *can't*

SCOPE AND SEQUENCE

Unit	Topics	Grammar
09 Where was he last night?	Past events	Simple past 1: *Be* verb; past progressive
10 What did you do yesterday?	Past events; holidays; traveling	Simple past 2: Regular/irregular verbs; wh-questions
11 How many apples do you need?	Food; recipes	Countable and uncountable nouns
12 I'd like to go rollerblading	Free time activities; likes and dislikes	Infinitives and gerunds
13 He's tall and funny	Describing things; describing people	Adjectives for describing people and things
14 I go jogging every day	Daily routines; habits; frequency	Adverbs of frequency; how often...?
15 What are you going to do tonight?	Future plans and activities	Future with *be going to* and *will*
16 Could you tell me how to get there?	Locations of places; directions	Imperatives

Speaking	Reading Writing	Listening Pronunciation
• Talking about past events using the past tense of *be* verb	• Writing about what other classmates did • Reading about what other people were doing	• Listening to find detailed information • Pronunciation of *was/wasn't/were/weren't*
• Talking about past events and holidays	• Reading about good places to go on the weekend • Writing a postcard to a friend	• Listening to a short biography of Tiger Woods • Pronunciation of ending sounds of simple past tense
• Talking about healthy foods • Talking about how to make food	• Writing about favorite foods • Reading about a recipe	• Listening for different types of foods and their quantifiers • Minimal pair: /p/ and /f/
• Talking about free time activities • Talking about how to decline requests	• Reading about different types of free time activities • Reading about likes and dislikes	• Listening to people talk about their free time activities • Pronunciation of *going to* and *want to*
• Describing things and people's physical appearance	• Reading about ideal types • Writing descriptions of things	• Listening for descriptions of things and people • Linking: and/or
• Talking about healthy habits and pastime activities	• Reading about how to live for a long time	• Listening for how often people do activities • Stressed and unstressed words
• Talking about future plans • Talking about and how to make suggestions	• Reading about New Year's resolutions • Writing about vacation plans	• Listening for future plans • Minimal pair: /l/ and /r/
• Asking about locations of places • Asking for directions	• Reading about people's favorite places • Writing about directions to places	• Listening for the directions to the places in a certain area • Word stress

Nice to meet you

Start

Practice saying the greetings.

 Great   Good   Not bad   Okay   Not so good   Terrible

Dialogue

Listen to the dialogue and practice.

John: Hi. My name is John Smith.
Amy: I'm Amy Pitt.
John: Nice to meet you.
Amy: Nice to meet you, too.
John: Where are you from?
Amy: I'm from England.
John: Really? I'm from England, too.

Grammar | Be verb: Yes/No questions

Positive

I	am	I'm	
You	are	You're	
He		He's	
She	is	She's	from Korea.
It		It's	
We		We're	
You	are	You're	
They		They're	

Negative

I	am not	
You	are not (aren't)	
He		
She	is not (isn't)	from Korea.
It		
We		
You	are not (aren't)	
They		

Yes/No questions

Am	I	
Are	you	
Is	he / she / it	from Korea?
Are	we / you / they	

Short answers

Yes,	you	are.	No,	you	are not (aren't).	
	I	am.		I	am not.	
	he / she / it	is		he / she / it	is not (isn't).	
	we / you / they	are		we / you / they	are not (aren't).	

✽ **Caution:** Yes, I am. (O) Yes, I'm. (X)

Speak 1 | Greetings

With your partner, practice the dialogue using the expressions below.

A: Hi. I'm _____.
B: Hello. My name is _____.
A: Nice to meet you.
B: Nice to meet you, too.

- Hi.
- Hello.
- How are you doing?
- Good morning / afternoon / evening.

- Nice to meet you.
- Glad to meet you.
- Nice meeting you.
- Good to see you.

Nice to meet you

Speak 2 | At a costume party

People are greeting each other at a party. Practice the dialogue.

A: Hello, I'm James Brown.
B: Hi, my name is Nancy Yang.
A: Where are you from?
B: I'm from Thailand. How about you?
A: I'm from Canada.

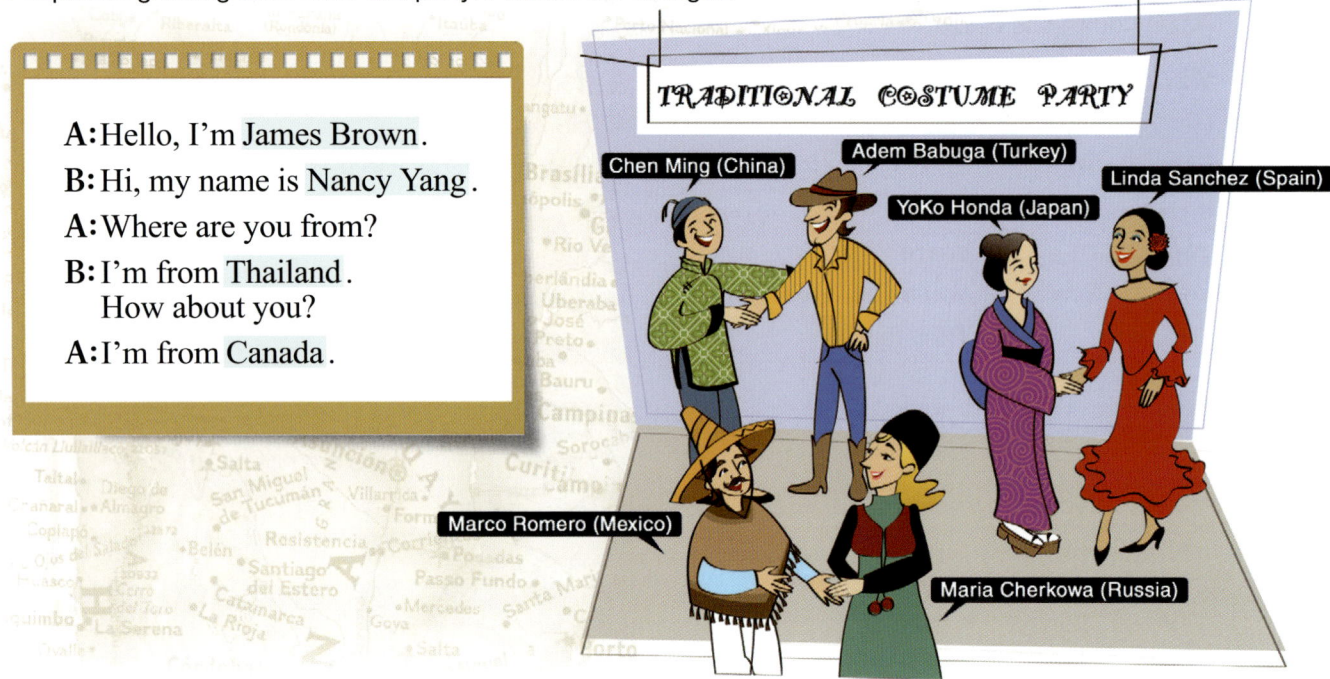

Speak 3 | Where are you from?

People are asking each other where they are from. Practice the dialogue.

A: Are you from the United States?
B: No, I'm not. I'm British.
A: Oh, are you from London?
B: Yes, I'm from London. / No, I'm from Manchester.

Chinese
Beijing/Shanghai

Italian
Rome/Venice

Japanese
Tokyo/Osaka

Canadian
Vancouver/Toronto

French
Paris/Lyon

Korean
Seoul/Pusan

Activity 1 | Interview

 Step 1 Choose two of your classmates. Interview them and fill out the interview forms. Use the sample questions below.

Questions
1. What is your first / last name?
2. How old are you?
3. Where are you from?
4. What do you do? (What is your job?)
5. What's your cell phone number?

01
1. First name:
   Last name:
2. Age:
3. Country:
4. Job / Occupation:
5. Cell phone number:

02
1. First name:
   Last name:
2. Age:
3. Country:
4. Job / Occupation:
5. Cell phone number:

 Step 2 Tell the class about one of the two classmates you interviewed. Follow the sample sentences below.

e.g. My partner's name is Mi Hee Kang.
She is 24 years old.
She is from Korea.
She is a teacher.
Her cell phone number is 011-928-3185.

Activity 2 | Find the mystery man

Work with a partner. Ask your partner to choose one of the pictures below but not to tell you which one.

❶ John (28)

❷ Jane (22)

❸ Brian (50)

❹ Maggie (37)

❺ Sue (16)

❻ Max (63)

❼ Kelly (71)

❽ Don (15)

Ask five questions to your partner and find out who the person is. See the example below.

Questions	Answers
Is he old?	No, he isn't.
Is his tie black?	No, it isn't.
Is his hair long?	No, it isn't.
Is his hair brown?	Yes, it is.
Is his name John?	Correct!

Did you get it right? Switch roles and play again.

Listen

Listen to the recordings and complete the table below.

Name of the caller	Phone number
Lisa	
Jon	
Alice	
Chris	

Pronunciation

Listen to the following words and underline the stressed part in each word.

Country	Nationality
Kor<u>e</u>a	Kor<u>e</u>an
Japan	Japanese
Canada	Canadian
China	Chinese
Italy	Italian
Germany	German
France	French
Thailand	Thai

Nice to meet you   13

UNIT 02

Who is she?

Start

Fill out the application form with the correct information from the list.

Word List

American
32 Walnut St. Irvine CA
949-321-1274
Female
Jennifer Roberts
25
92602
Nov 16, 1981
Singer
jroberts@kmail.com

Application Form

First Name:	
Last Name:	
Age:	Birthdate:
Gender:	
Nationality:	
Address:	
Zip code:	
Occupation:	
Email address:	
Phone number:	

Dialogue

Listen to the dialogue and practice.

Chris: Who is she?
Pete: She is my cousin, Christine.
Chris: What is her job?
Pete: She is a math teacher.
Chris: That's good! What is her phone number?
Pete: Come on, you'll have to ask her.

Grammar | Be verb: Wh-questions

Wh-questions			Answers
Who	is	she?	She is Dona Morris.
What	is	her phone number?	It is 321-1274.
When	is	her birthday?	It is November 16th.
Where	is	she from?	She's from Canada.
What	is	her nationality?	She is Canadian.
What color	is	her hair?	It's black.
How old	is	she?	She's 29 years old.
How tall	is	she?	She is 162cm tall.

Speak 1 | A personal record

Look at the personal record of James Brown. Talk about it with your partner. See the example below.

Personal Record

Name: James Brown
Date of birth: August 26, 1976
Nationality: Australian
Job: Mechanic
Work address: 1755 Broadway, New York, NY
Home address: 359 Maple Street, Queens, NY
Email address: jamesbrown@inet.com
Cell phone number: 646-321-1275

A: What is his cell phone number?
B: It's 646-321-1275.
A: When is his birthday?
B: It's August 26th.

Who is she?

Speak 2 | Upcoming events

Two people are talking about some upcoming events. Practice the dialogue looking at the memo below.

A: When is Jane's birthday party?
B: It is October 3rd.
A: What day is it?
B: It's Wednesday.

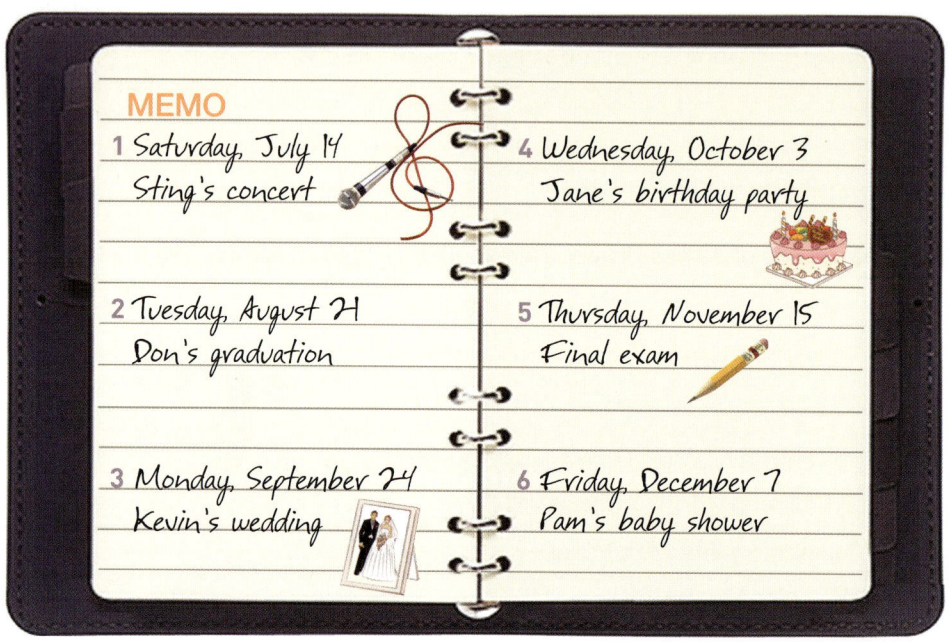

MEMO
1 Saturday, July 14 — Sting's concert
2 Tuesday, August 21 — Don's graduation
3 Monday, September 24 — Kevin's wedding
4 Wednesday, October 3 — Jane's birthday party
5 Thursday, November 15 — Final exam
6 Friday, December 7 — Pam's baby shower

Speak 3 | What is he like?

Using the information given, talk about what these two people are like.

How old is he?
He is _____ years old.

How tall is he?
He is _____ cm tall.

What color is his hair?
It is _____.

Age: 26
Height: 163cm
Hair: black

Age: 23
Height: 178cm
Hair: brown

Activity 1 | Who are they?

Student A

Step 1 You are missing some information about the people below. Your partner has the information that you don't have. Fill in the chart by asking your partner questions.

Questions
How old is Jack Windsor?
When is his birthday?
How tall is he?
What's his nationality?
What is his favorite food?

Answers
He is 69 years old.
It is April 22nd.
He is 175cm tall.
He is American.
It's sushi.

- Age
- Birthday
- Height
- Nationality
- Favorite food

1 Pamela Diaz
- 34
- Aug. 30
- 174cm
- American
- nachos

2 Brad Grant

3 Jaomin Li
- 41
- Dec. 31
- 170cm
- Chinese
- dim sum

4 Tim Woods

5 Jina Kim
- 20
- Nov. 5
- 162cm
- Korean
- bulgogi

6 David Anderson

Step 2 When you're finished, check your answers with your partner.

Activity 1 | Who are they?   Student B

Step 1 You are missing some information about the people below. Your partner has the information that you don't have. Fill in the chart by asking your partner questions.

Questions
How old is Jack Windsor?
When is his birthday?
How tall is he?
What is his nationlaity?
What is his favorite food?

Answers
He is 69 years old.
It is April 22nd.
He is 175cm tall.
He is American.
It's sushi.

- Age
- Birthday
- Height
- Nationality
- Favorite food

1 Pamela Diaz

2 Brad Grant
- 46
- Sept. 9
- 180cm
- British
- fish and chips

3 Jaomin Li

4 Tim Woods
- 31
- Dec. 30
- 188cm
- Canadian
- steak

5 Jina Kim

6 David Anderson
- 31
- May 2
- 174cm
- Australian
- bagels

Step 2 When you're finished, check your answers with your partner.

Listen

Listen to the six sentences. They are the responses to the questions on the left. Match each response with the correct question.

When is Christmas?   •   ①

What's his nationality?   •   ②

What color is your shirt?   •   ③

Who is your favorite actor?   •   ④

How big is John's car?   •   ⑤

What time is lunch?   •   ⑥

Pronunciation

A. Listen to the words and circle the correct ending of each word.

1 -teen   -ty
2 -teen   -ty
3 -teen   -ty
4 -teen   -ty

B. Listen to the following numbers and choose the correct spelling of each number from the list below.

1 12th .... [twelfθ]

2 21st .... [twentifə́ːrst]

3 3rd .... [θəːrd]

4 32nd .... [θəːrti séknd]

5 55th .... [fifti fífθ]

> twenty-first,   thirty-second,   twelfth,   third,   fifty-fifth

Who is she?   19

There is a cell phone on the table

Start

Below is a list of things in a house. Which room does each item belong in? Put the words under the correct headings.

Item list

- lamp
- bed
- bookcase
- dining table
- pillow
- sink
- sofa/couch
- shower
- toilet
- coffee table
- television
- stove
- refrigerator
- bathtub
- dresser
- rug

Bedroom	Living room	Kitchen	Bathroom

Dialogue

Listen to the dialogue and practice.

Lisa: What's in this box?
Tom: It's your birthday present. Open it.
Lisa: Oh, it's a lipstick.
Tom: Do you like it?
Lisa: Yes, very much. This is my favorite color.
Tom: I'm glad you like it.
Lisa: Thank you for the gift!

Grammar | Regular and irregular plural nouns / Prepositions

Regular plural nouns			Irregular plural nouns
Singular noun **+s**		map - maps	man - men
-s/-sh/-ch/-x	**+es**	dish - dishes	mouse - mice
consonant + y	**- ies**	lady - ladies	tooth - teeth
vowel + y	**+s**	key - keys	fish - fish
-f/-fe	**- ves**	knife - knives	child - children

There is... / There are...

There is a sofa in the living room.
Is there a sofa in the living room?
→ Yes, there is. / No, there isn't.

There are two sofas in the living room.
Are there two sofas in the living room?
→ Yes, there are. / No, there aren't.

Prepositions of place

 in
 on
 under
 next to
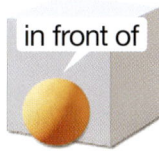 in front of
 behind

Speak 1 | In the bag

There are some items in the bags. Talk about what items are in the bags.

What's in Jane's bag?
What's in Danny's bag?

There is a pen.   There are two pens.

Jane's bag: glasses, wallet, mirror, lipsticks, pen

Danny's bag: keys, cell phone, notebooks, pens, pencils

There is a cell phone on the table

Speak 2 | In the living room

People are talking about household items. Practice the dialogue.

A: Is there a rug in the living room?
B: Yes, there is.
A: Are there any slippers in the bedroom?
B: No, there aren't.

In the bedroom	In the living room	In the kitchen
a bed ⭕	a rug ⭕	a microwave oven ⭕
a dresser ❌	an armchair ❌	a dishwasher ❌
pillows ⭕	cushions ⭕	chairs ⭕
slippers ❌	paintings ❌	a cupboard ❌

Speak 3 | In the office

You are looking for things in an office. With your partner, take turns asking and answering questions about where the items are.

A: Where is the trashcan?
B: It is **under** the desk.
A: Then, where are the pens?
B: They are **on** the desk.

22 UNIT 03

Activity 1 | Spot the differences

 Look at the two pictures and locate the items from the list below. Then complete the chart.

	In picture 1	In picture 2
The bag is	on the bed	under the bed
The cats are		
The hangers are		
The basketball is		
The glasses are		
The cell phone is		

 Compare your chart with those of your classmates.

 Write a description of one of the pictures using 'There is~' or 'There are~'.

Example

In picture 1, there is a bag on the bed. There are two books on the dresser.

Activity 2 | My dream house

 Step 1 Think of your dream house. Then with your partner, talk about it by asking and answering the questions below.

apartment   **mansion**   **ranch house**   **townhouse**

What is your dream house?

How many rooms are there?

What kinds of rooms are there?

What is in each room?

 Step 2 Write about your dream house.

My dream house is a _____.

There is / are _____ room(s) in the house.

There are _____ bedroom(s), _____ bathroom(s), _____ living room(s), _____ kitchen(s) and _____.

There is/are _____, _____, and _____ in the bed room, _____ in the living room, and _____ in the bathroom.

Also, there is/are _____ in the kitchen.

24 UNIT 03

Listen

Listen to the descriptions of the house and check (✓) whether each sentence is correct or incorrect.

	C	I		C	I		C	I
1			3			5		
2			4			6		

Pronunciation

Listen to each word and put it into the appropriate category according to the final 's' sound.

	/s/	/z/	/iz/
e.g.	desks	movies	benches
1			
2			
3			
4			
5			
6			
7			
8			

| newspapers | cameras | clocks | watches |
| purses | keys | stamps | rugs |

UNIT 04 That's mine!

Start

Find the correct names of the items from the two lists below and write them under the pictures.

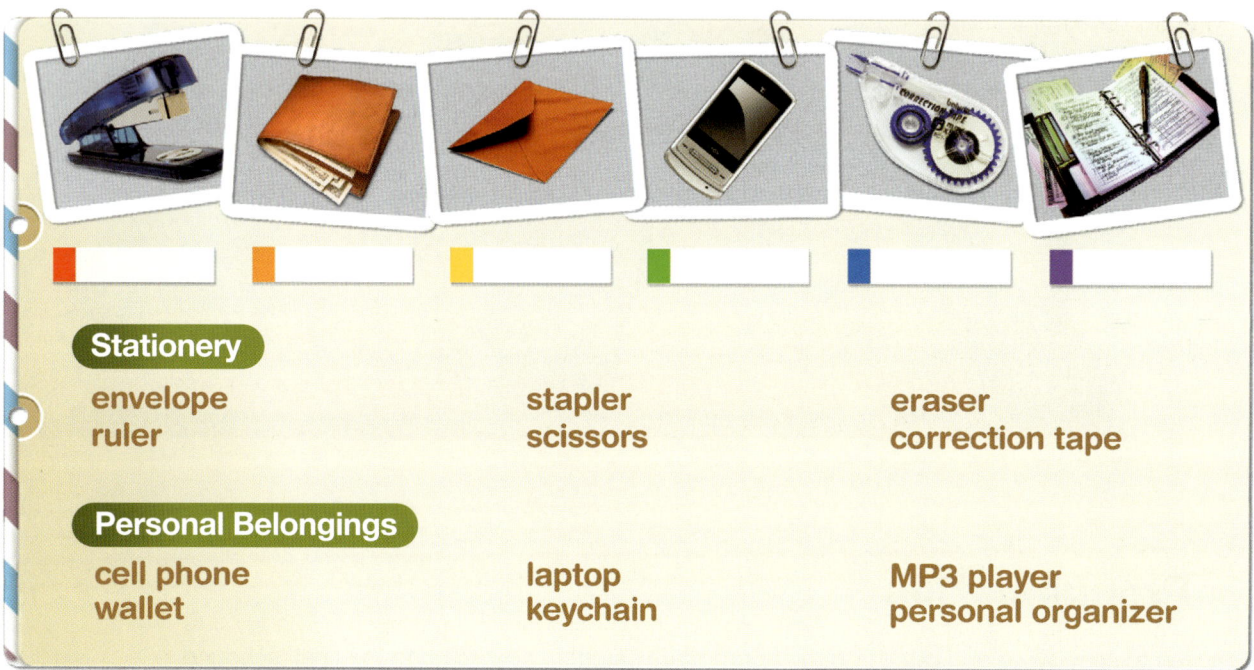

Stationery
envelope   stapler   eraser
ruler   scissors   correction tape

Personal Belongings
cell phone   laptop   MP3 player
wallet   keychain   personal organizer

Dialogue

Listen to the dialogue and practice.

Eric: James, is this your car?
James: No, it's not mine.
Eric: Then whose is it?
James: It's Kevin's new car.
Eric: Oh, really? Cool.
James: Yes, it is.

Grammar | Subject pronouns / Possessives

Subject pronouns		Possessive adjectives		Possessive pronouns	
Singular	Plural	Singular	Plural	Singular	Plural
I	we	my	our	mine	ours
you	you	your	your	yours	yours
he	they	his	their	his	theirs
she		her		hers	
it		its		X	

Whose (pen) is this?
- It's my pen.
- It's mine.

Whose (pens) are these?
- They're Jane's pens.
- They're Jane's.

Caution!
I have a cat. <u>Its</u> name is Kate.
I have a cat. <u>It's</u> Kate.

Speak 1 | That's my wallet

With a partner, practice the dialogue using the items below.

A: Is this your wallet?
B: Yes, it is.
A: What about that one?
B: It's Sam's.

A: Are these your wallets?
B: Yes, they are.
A: What about those ones?
B: They're Wendy's.

❶ cell phone–Brandy's

❷ cap–Kevin's

❸ earrings–Amanda's

❹ mirror–Joanne's

❺ pens–Jake's

❻ glasses–Peter's

Speak 2 | Shopping spree

Four housemates (Ann, Jane, Tom, and Don) went shopping together and just came back. Now, they're sorting out what they bought. Practice the dialogues using the information in the table.

What they bought				
Ann	an electric dictionary	a lipstick	earrings	paper clips
Jane	sunglasses	a necklace	correction pens	high heels
Tom	sneakers	a wristwatch	a backpack	an MP3 player
Don	socks	envelopes	hiking boots	a personal organizer

A: Is this your lipstick?
B: No, it's not mine.
A: Then whose lipstick is this?
B: It's Ann's.

A: Is that your lipstick?
B: No, it's not mine.
A: Then whose lipstick is it?
B: It's Ann's.

A: Are these your sunglasses?
B: No, they aren't.
A: Then whose sunglasses are they?
B: They're Jane's.

A: Are those your sunglasses?
B: No, they aren't.
A: Then whose sunglasses are they?
B: They're Jane's.

Activity 1 | Family tree

 Step 1 This is a family tree. Study how the people are related. Then answer the questions filling in the blanks with the correct words from the list.

husband	wife	son	daughter	cousin
niece	aunt	uncle	grandmother	grandfather
father-in-law	mother-in-law	sister-in-law	brother-in-law	grandson

1 Who is Pam? She is Tom's _____.
2 Who is Nick? He is _____ husband.
3 Who is Nicole? She is Jack's _____.
4 Who is Joe? He is Kevin's _____.
5 Who is Jane? She is _____ sister.
6 Who is Tom? He is Debby's _____.
7 Who is Debby? She is Pam's _____.
8 Who is Jack? He is _____ son-in-law.

 Step 2 Compare your answers with your classmates.

Activity 2 | Whose is this?

 Step 1 Peter, Brad, and Jane are on a camping trip in the mountains. Check who the items belong to and complete the following dialogue by filling in the blanks.

Jane: Brad, is this _____ flashlight?
Brad: No, it's not _____. I guess it's _____.
Jane: Peter, can I use _____ flashlight for a minute?
Peter: Sure. _____ towels are those? Are they _____, Brad?
Brad: No, they're not _____. They're _____.
Peter: _____. Can I borrow one of _____ towels?
Jane: Go ahead.
Peter: Brad, are these _____ hiking boots?
Brad: Yes, they are _____.
Jane: Oh, I like them a lot.
Peter: I like them, too. They look light and fashionable.
Brad: Thanks. I got them for 30 dollars.
Jane: It's getting chilly. I feel cold.
Brad: Put on _____ windbreaker. Here you are.
Jane: Thanks a lot. You're very kind. Peter, is this mug _____?
Peter: No, it's not _____. Actually it's _____.

 Step 2 Work with a partner. Make up your own dialogue based on the one above.

Listen

Listen to two people asking and answering questions. Check (✓) **R** if the answer is right. Check (✓) **W** if the answer is wrong.

Dialogue	R	W
1		
2		
3		
4		
5		
6		
7		
8		

Pronunciation

A. Listen and circle the sentence you hear.

1. ⓐ Eat your apple.
   ⓑ Eat your apples.

2. ⓐ Look at the dog.
   ⓑ Look at the dogs.

3. ⓐ Clean the room.
   ⓑ Clean the rooms.

4. ⓐ Pick up the pencil.
   ⓑ Pick up the pencils.

5. ⓐ Did you fill the tank?
   ⓑ Did you fill the tanks?

6. ⓐ Wash the car.
   ⓑ Wash the cars.

7. ⓐ Can you see the picture?
   ⓑ Can you see the pictures?

8. ⓐ Did you meet his sister?
   ⓑ Did you meet his sisters?

B. Listen and fill in the blanks.

1. Brad is _____ best friend. I like _____ personality.
2. Jason loves _____ dog. _____ name is Piggy.
3. Kate and _____ husband like shopping.
4. Maggie's family have _____ own house.
5. You look great. I like _____ hairstyle.

UNIT 05 What are you doing?

Start

Match the verbs on the left with the words on the right to make expressions about daily activities.

1. watch
2. ride
3. play
4. take
5. go
6. listen
7. do
8. put on

a. a shower
b. to the movies
c. to music
d. the dishes
e. TV
f. a bicycle
g. the piano
h. makeup

Dialogue

Listen to the dialogue and practice.

Tim: Hey, James! What are you doing?
James: I'm playing tennis.
Tim: Tennis?
James: Yeah, I'm taking a tennis class this semester.
TimA: Oh, sounds fun.
James: I enjoy playing it. By the way, where are you going?
Tim: I'm going to the library. I have a math midterm exam this Friday.
James: Good luck!

Grammar | Present progressive

Are you study**ing** now?
- Yes, I am.
- No, I'm not. **I'm** watch**ing** a movie.

Caution!
have → having
swim → swimming

What **are** you do**ing**? I'm hav**ing** dinner.
What **is** Kate do**ing**? She's listen**ing** to music.
What **are** Sue and Brad do**ing**? They're play**ing** tennis.

Speak 1 | Are you studying?

With your partner, practice the dialogues.

A: Are you studying?
B: No, I'm not.
   I am reading.

A: Is Cecil studying?
B: No, she isn't.
   She is singing.

A: Are Pam and Nick studying?
B: No, they aren't.
   They are cooking.

1. Kate
2. Tim and Jane
3. your roommate
4. Jack and Pete
5. the students
6. Tom's dog

✗ have dinner with friends
✗ watch TV
✗ play computer games
✗ cook dinner
✗ dance together
✗ run in the yard

⊙ read a book
⊙ clean the house
⊙ play basketball
⊙ work out at the gym
⊙ sing together
⊙ sleep in its house

Speak 2 | What time is it there?

You are calling friends in other countries. Ask them what time it is and what they are doing.

A: Hello, Jane?
B: Hi, Susan.
A: What time is it in LA?
B: It's ten in the morning.
A: What are you doing?
B: I'm reading the newspaper.

Tokyo	Seoul	Moscow	London	New York	Hawaii
06:00 AM	12:00 PM	12:00 PM	08:00 PM	09:00 PM	02:00 AM
Mary	James	Kim	Chris	Anna	Peter

1. Mary | swim
2. James | walk in the park
3. Kim | listen to music
4. Chris | talk to a friend on Messenger
5. Anna | watch TV
6. Peter | fix the bicycle

Speak 3 | What are you doing?

People are on a college campus. With your partner, talk about where each person is and what he or she is doing. Use the expressions from the list.

A: Where's Kate?
B: She's in the computer room.
A: What's she doing?
B: She's checking her emails.

library: Jason

locker room: Christine

computer room: Kate

language lab: Maria

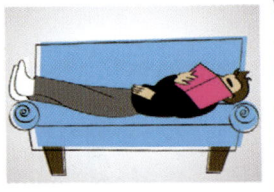
Dormitory room: Kevin

cafeteria: Scott

study for the final exam   put her bag in the locker   check emails
practice English   sleep on a couch   drink coffee

Activity 1 | On the street

 Step 1 Look at the people in the picture and write about what each person is doing.

1. Alice is dancing in the street.
2. Peter _____ with his girlfriend.
3. _____
4. _____
5. _____
6. _____

 Step 2 Look at the picture again. Answer the following questions about what each person is doing.

> **e.g.** Is Alice dancing with her friend? → No, she isn't. She is dancing alone.

1. Is Peter eating a hamburger? → _____
2. Is Michael lying on a bench? → _____
3. Is Drew eating ice cream in the café? → _____
4. Is Nick playing the piano? → _____
5. Is Jack having a dessert in the restaurant? → _____

What are you doing? 35

Activity 2 | Text messages

 Step 1 Two college students are exchanging text messages on their cell phones. Read the messages and answer the questions in full sentences.

[Phone 1 - Diana to Chris]
Chris,
Where are you?
I'm writing a term paper at the library.
Let's have lunch together at the Sweet Deli.

[Phone 2 - Chris to Diana]
Hey, Diana...
I'm waiting for Dr. Kim at his office. I'm reading the textbook for history class. Having lunch sounds good to me. Is Andy there, too?

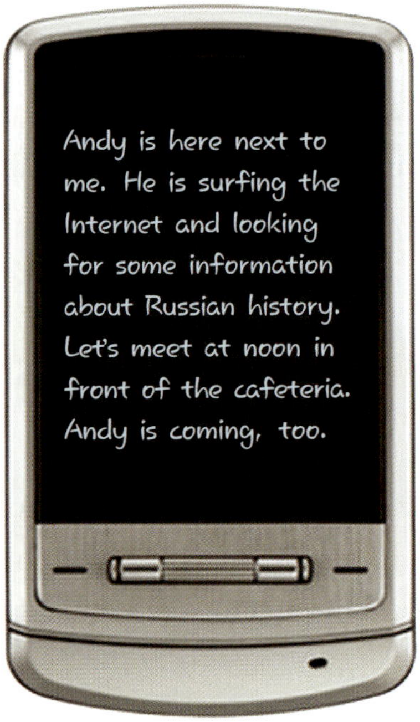

[Phone 3 - Chris to Diana]
Andy is here next to me. He is surfing the Internet and looking for some information about Russian history. Let's meet at noon in front of the cafeteria. Andy is coming, too.

[Phone 4 - Diana to Chris]
OK.
I'm in the mood for pasta.
How about you guys?
Anyway,
See you soon.
Bye.

1. Who are exchanging the text messages?
2. What is Chris doing?
3. Where is Diana waiting for Dr. Kim?
4. What is Andy doing?

36 UNIT 05

Listen

Listen to each short conversation. Then choose the correct answer to the question.

Q1 What is Sue doing in the office?
 ⓐ Working on the computer
 ⓑ Talking on the phone

Q2 What is Ted having?
 ⓐ A sandwich
 ⓑ A hamburger

Q3 Where are Susie and Jacob going?
 ⓐ To the hospital
 ⓑ To the gym

Q4 What is Maria making?
 ⓐ Coffee
 ⓑ Tea

Pronunciation

Listen to the questions and check (✓) whether the intonation is rising or falling.

	Rising	Falling
1		
2		
3		
4		
5		
6		
7		
8		

UNIT 06 Does he go to work early?

Start

What do you like to do in your free time? Here are some activities that you can do. Match each expression with the correct picture.

- cook
- read
- go hiking
- go shopping
- listen to music
- ride a bicycle
- work out at the gym
- walk the dog

Dialogue

Listen to the dialogue and practice.

Julia: What do you do on Sundays?
Pam: I usually go hiking. How about you?
Julia: Well, I sleep in and do some housework.
Pam: Then do you ever go out?
Julia: Sometimes I go to the movies.
Pam: By the way, does your brother still train for marathons?
Julia: Yes, he does.
Pam: Great! I'd like to train with him.

Grammar | Simple present 1

I
You
They
Jon and Kate
} **watch** TV.
don't watch TV.

He
She
My dog
} **watches** TV.
doesn't watch TV.

Do you watch TV?
- Yes, I do.
- No, I don't.

Does Brad watch TV?
- Yes, he does.
- No, he doesn't.

3rd person singular

* **verbs with endings**
  -s, -sh, -ch, **+es**
  brush — brushes
  watch — watches

* **Irregular singular verbs**
  have — has
  do — does
  go — goes

Speak 1 | Daily routines

Look at the daily schedules and talk about them with a partner.

My day
- 08:00   get up / brush my teeth
- 09:00   leave for school
- 03:00   study at the library
- 06:00   get home
- 08:00   do yoga
- 11:00   go to bed

Sam's day
- 09:00   get up / take a shower
- 09:30   go for a run
- 10:30   go to work
- 08:00   have dinner
- 09:00   watch TV
- 12:00   go to sleep

A: Do you get up early?
B: No, I don't.
A: Then what time do you get up?
B: I get up at 8.
A: What do you do after that?
B: I leave for school at... Then

A: Does Sam get up early?
B: No, he doesn't.
A: Then what time does he get up?
B: He gets up at 9 and...
A: What does he do after that?
B: He... Then

Speak 2 | Free-time activities

With a partner, talk about what people do in their free time using the information given.

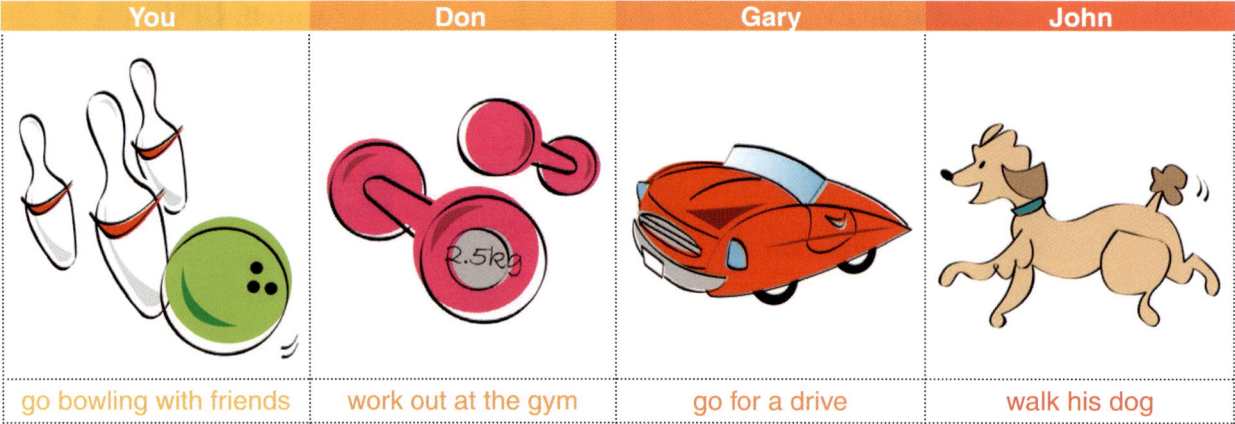

You	Don	Gary	John
go bowling with friends	work out at the gym	go for a drive	walk his dog

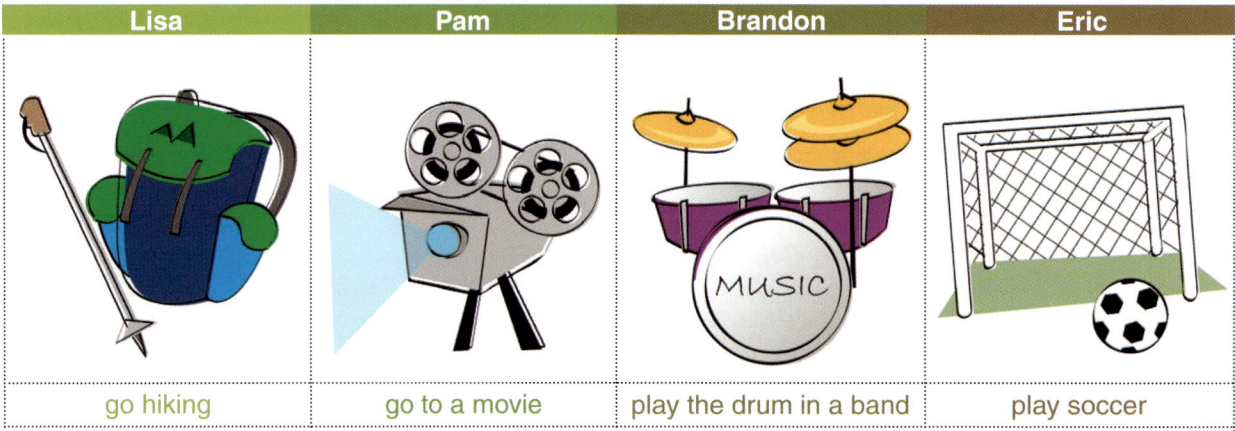

Lisa	Pam	Brandon	Eric
go hiking	go to a movie	play the drum in a band	play soccer

A: What do you do in your free time?
B: I usually get some rest at home.

A: What does he do in his free time?
B: He goes for a walk in the park.

Activity 1 | Daily routine

 Read the dialogue.

> A: Anna, you look very busy everyday.
>
> B: Yeah, I'm busy with many things.
>
> A: What's your day like?
>
> B: I get up at 6 and go for a walk for 30 minutes. After that I take a shower, put on makeup, and get dressed.
>
> A: What about breakfast?
>
> B: I don't have breakfast at home. I usually leave for work at 7:30 and get to work at 8. On my way to work, I drop by Wendy's, get some breakfast to go, and then have it at the office.
>
> A: And then do you start work?
>
> B: Yes, I start work around 8:30. I have many meetings in the morning.
>
> A: Oh, You must be busy. What time do you get off?
>
> B: I get off at 6:30.
>
> A: Then do you go straight home?
>
> B: Yeah, I arrive home at 7 and cook dinner. After dinner, I read the newspaper, watch TV, and go to bed at 10:30.
>
> A: Sounds like you're an early bird!

 With a partner, talk about Anna's daily routine using the questions below.

1. What time does she go to work?
2. What does she do after taking a shower?
3. Does she have breakfast at home?
4. Does she go straight home after work?
5. What time does she go to bed?

 Write about your own daily routine.

Activity 2 | The things I like to do

 Step 1 Work with a partner. Pretend you are Pete and Lynn. Talk about the things you like to do in your free time. Use the information given and follow the sample dialogue.

> Pete: Do you like sports?
> Lynn: Yes, I do.
> Pete: What kind of sports do you like?
> Lynn: I like tennis. What about you? Do you like sports?
> Pete: Of course. Actually, I like watching sports.
> Lynn: What sports do you watch?
> Pete: I usually watch soccer and basketball games. I sometimes go to the games.

Music
- pop music
- listening to classical music.
- listen to Chopin's piano concertos.
- go to concerts.

Movies
- romantic comedies
- watching DVDs
- watch horror movies
- buy DVDs.

Books
- novels
- reading comic books
- read Garfield
- read the Spiderman series

TV shows
- soap operas
- watching talk shows
- watch the Oprah Winfrey show
- videotape the shows

 Step 2 Work in pairs. Have the same conversation using your own information.

Listen

Listen to the conversations and check (✓) if each statement is true or false.

		True	False
1	Jason usually stays late at the office.		
2	Mary really loves shopping.		
3	Brian likes walking rather than driving.		
4	Mr. and Mrs. Diaz usually go hiking on the weekend.		

Pronunciation

Listen to each word and check (✓) the ending sound you hear.

	/s/	/z/	/iz/
1			
2			
3			
4			
5			
6			
7			
8			

UNIT 07 What does she do?

Start

Choose the correct job title for each person and write the word under the picture.

- firefighter
- baker
- cashier
- photographer
- accountant
- hairdresser
- flight attendant
- cook

Dialogue

Listen to the dialogue and practice.

Kelly: Hey, Chris. How's it going?
Chris: Good. I got a new job.
Kelly: Oh, really? What do you do exactly?
Chris: I teach science at Maryland Middle School.
Kelly: That's great. How do you like it?
Chris: So far, so good.
Kelly: How long does it take to get to work?
Chris: About 20 minutes.
Kelly: Not bad.

Grammar | Simple present 2: Wh-questions

Wh - questions

What does she do?
What company does she work for?
When does she go to work?
What time does she have lunch?
Where does she live?
Who does she have lunch with?
How does she get to work?

Answers

She is an office worker.
She works for AT&T.
She goes to work at 8:30.
She has lunch at 1:00.
She lives in Texas.
She has lunch with her coworkers.
She takes the bus to work.

Speak 1 | What do they do?

With your partner, talk about the fishing club members' jobs.

A: What does Peter do?
B: He's a teacher.
A: Who does he work for?
B: He works for Long Beach Middle School.

List of Members

Go & Catch Fishing Club

Name	Occupation	Company
Jack	accountant	H&H Trading
Tom	firefighter	the LA Fire Department
Susan	nurse	Saint Mary's Hospital
Jason	college student	UCC
Andy	fashion designer	Prime Boutique
Mr. & Mrs. Kim	travel agents	Joy Travel

Speak 2 | What's his day like?

With your partner, talk about Eric and Julie's daily schedules. Follow the example dialogue.

> A: **What time** does he leave for work?
> B: He leaves for work at 7:30.
> A: **When** does he get home?
> B: He gets home around 6:00.

Eric's daily schedule

| 07:30 AM | 08:30 AM | 09:30 AM | 12:00 PM | 05:30 PM |
| leave for work | get to work | have a meeting | have lunch | get off work |

Anna's daily schedule

| 08:00 AM | 09:30 AM | 11:30 AM | 02:00 PM | 04:30 PM | 06:00 PM |
| leave for school | get to school | have lunch | have a piano lesson | finish school | get home |

Speak 3 | The way to work

With your partner, talk about how the people go to work and how long it takes. Follow the example dialogue.

> A: **Where** does Kevin live?
> B: He lives near the lake.
> A: **How** does he get to work?
> B: He takes the subway.
> A: **How long** does it take him to get to work?
> B: It takes him about 30 minutes.

❶ Brad lives near the stadium. He takes the bus to work. It takes 40 minutes.

❷ Jennifer lives near the beach. She drives to work. It takes 30 minutes.

❸ Andy and Drew live near the park. They walk to work. It takes 20 minutes.

❹ Janice lives near the airport. She rides a bicycle to work. It takes 15 minutes.

Activity 1 | What do they do?

Student A

Step 1 Ask your partner for the missing information about the people. Follow the example, then, fill in the blanks.

> **Example**
>
> Q: What does Michelle do? → A: She is a Web designer.
> Q: What do web designers do? → A: They design Web sites.
> Q: What days does she work? → A: She works Monday through Friday.
> Q: Where does she work? → A: She works at home.

Daniel Frazer
- carpenter
-
- from Mon. to
- at

Amy Roberts
-
- at a restaurant
- ,   , Wed.
- at The Olive Garden

Brian Grant
-
- fix people's teeth
-
- at

Step 2 Your partner will ask you questions about the people below. Answer the questions with the information you have.

Cathy Jackson
- nurse
- take care of patients
- Mon., Wed., Fri.
- at Hopkins Hospital

Timothy Dane
- car dealer
- sell cars
- Mon. through Sat.
- at Best Automobiles

Joanne Lopez
- chef
- cook food
- Mon. through Fri.
- at Nice Grill

What does she do? 47

Activity 2 | What do they do?   Student B

 Step 1 Your partner will ask you questions about the people below. Answer the questions with the information you have. See the example below.

Example

Q: What does Michelle do? → A: She is a web designer.
Q: What do web designers do? → A: They make designs for web sites.
Q: What days does she work? → A: She works Monday through Friday.
Q: Where does she work? → A: She works at home.

Daniel Frazer
- carpenter
- build furniture and houses
- from Mon. to Thu.
- at Best Carpenter's Shop

Amy Roberts
- waitress
- serve food at a restaurant
- Mon., Tue., Wed.
- at The Olive Garden

Brian Grant
- dentist
- fix people's teeth
- Mon. through Fri.
- at Central Hospital

 Step 2 Ask your partner for the missing information about the people. Fill in the blanks with the information you get from your partner.

Cathy Jackson
- _____
- _____ patients
- Mon., _____, _____
- at Hopkins Hospital

Timothy Dane
- car dealer
- _____
- Mon. through _____
- at _____ Automobiles

Joanne Lopez
- _____
- _____
- Mon. through _____
- at _____ Grill

48   UNIT 07

Listen

Listen to four short conversations and choose the correct answer for each question.

Conversation 1

Q What sport does Alice play?
- ⓐ soccer
- ⓑ swimming
- ⓒ tennis

Conversation 2

Q What language do Peter and Nancy study?
- ⓐ French
- ⓑ Japanese
- ⓒ Chinese

Conversation 3

Q What kind of food does David have for lunch?
- ⓐ Korean food
- ⓑ Vietnamese food
- ⓒ Fast food

Conversation 4

Q Which group of friends does Tony practice dancing with?
- ⓐ friends from the dancing club
- ⓑ friends from school
- ⓒ friends from his hometown

Pronunciation

Listen to the questions and complete them by filling in the blanks.

1 (   ) do on the weekend?
2 (   ) have for lunch?
3 (   ) want to live?
4 (   ) play tennis with?
5 (   ) stay during the vacation?
6 (   ) have in your pockets?

UNIT 08

Can you dance well?

Start

What can you do? Check all the activities that you can do.

 play the guitar
 play tennis
 dance
 swim

 drive
 snowboard
 speak English
 paint

 rollerblade
 type

What else can you do? Talk about these abilities with your partner.

Dialogue

Listen to the dialogue and practice.

Susan: Jeremy, can you help me with this?
Jeremy: Sure. What is it?
Susan: I just can't understand what these words mean.
Jeremy: Oh, they mean, "I love you" in French.
Susan: Wow! Can you speak French?
Jeremy: I'm not good at speaking it, but I can read a little.
Susan: Anyway, thanks a lot.

Grammar | Can for ability

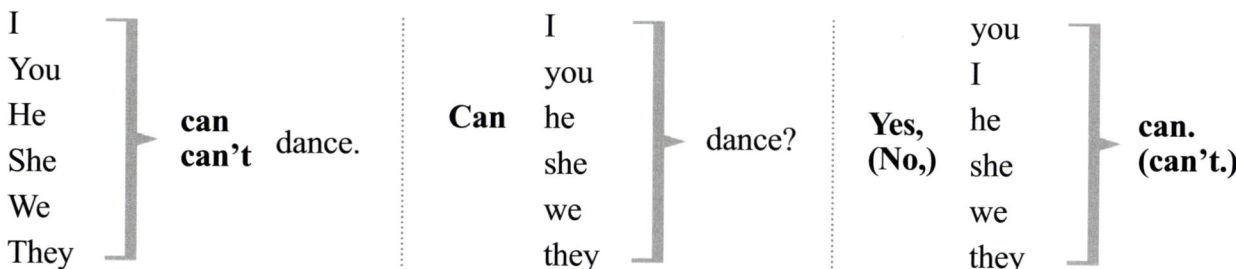

Can in wh-questions

What can I see at the zoo?
You can see many kinds of animals.

Where can I get a ticket?
You can get one at the ticket booth.

When can I get in?
You can get in at 10 a.m.

How can I get there?
You can get there by subway.

Can for requests

Can you close the door?
→ Sure. / No problem.

Can you help me?
→ Sorry.
   I'm on the phone right now.

Speak 1 | Can you play the guitar?

Practice the dialogue using the information given below.

Can you play the guitar?

No, I can't, but I can play the piano.

Well, only a little, but I'm good at playing the piano.

You	Fred	Amanda	Alex
play tennis △	swim ✗	dance ✗	play chess △
play badminton ☺	ski ☺	sing ☺	play cards ☺

☺ I can. / I'm good at it.   △ Only a little.   ✗ I can't.

Can you dance well? 51

Speak 2 | Ask Jessica

Work in pairs. Take turns both being Jessica and asking Jessica where you can do the things below. When you play the role of Jessica, answer the questions using the information below.

Where can I...
1 have a nice dinner
2 borrow books
3 get a haircut?
4 buy groceries?

A: **Where** can I mail this letter?
B: At the post office.
A: And **how** can I get there?
B: You can take the bus. It's near the city hall.

Jessica's Favorite Places

Sunset Dinner: behind the city hall / 10 min. by bus
The Civic Library: near the museum / 10 min. by taxi
Le Beauty: next to Central Station / 20 min. by subway
Kim's Market: behind the post office / a five-minute walk

Speak 3 | Can you do me a favor?

1 Match the sentences on the left with the proper phrases on the right.

I'm thirsty. •   • turn off the heater
It's heavy. •   • get me some water
I'm busy. •   • give me a hand
I'm sad. •   • copy this report
It's hot. •   • tell a funny story

2 With your partner, practice making requests and responding to them using the information above.

A: Can you do me a favor?
B: Sure. What is it?
A: I am so cold. Can you turn on the heater, please?
B: No problem. / Sorry. I'm on the phone right now.

Activity 1 | What are you good at?

 Step 1 Mark each activity in the list with the proper symbol given below.

- 😊 I'm good at …
- ◎ I can …
- △ Only a little.

swim	play table tennis
ski	play badminton
rollerblade	play the piano
snowboard	play the guitar
bowl	play the drum
play tennis	play pool
play baseball	dance
play football	sing
speak English/Chinese/Japanese	play computer games
make homepages	cook
ride a bicycle	bake

 Step 2 Now, with a partner, talk about the activities above using the questions below.

Questions
Can you …?

Are you good at …?
What are you good at?
What sports/musical instruments can you play?

Answers
Yes, I can. / No, I can't.
Yes, but only a little.
Yes, I am. / No, I'm not.
I'm good at …
I can play baseball / the piano.

Can you dance well? 53

Activity 2 | Classified ads

Step 1 Read the following advertisements.

Bay Sports Center

Want to be good at bowling? You can become a good bowler at the Bay Sports Center! Call now! 1-800-888-0505.

Jack's Golf Academy

Everyone can be an excellent golfer with a little money. We provide you with the best quality lessons. Open from 9 a.m. to 6 p.m.

Prime Acting School

Are you interested in acting? Come and learn at Prime Acting School. You can become a good actor. Our school is located downtown. Call now! 1-800-999-2345.

Orange County Jazz Academy

Do you want to learn how to sing jazz? Visit us. We will show you how to be a jazz singer. Located between Broadway and 32nd.

Daniel's Dancing Club

Daniel knows how to dance. You can be a great dancer, too! Please visit us. It's free! Open from 10 a.m. to 4 p.m. weekdays.

EASY MAGIC ACADEMY

Magic can make your life more interesting. We can teach you how to do magical tricks. You can become a magician. Call now. 1-800-646-3506

Step 2 With a partner, make up dialogues using the information in the ads above. Follow the example dialogue.

Example

A: Can you give me some good advice?

B: Sure, what's up?

A: You're a good actor. Where can I learn how to act?

B: You can try Prime Acting School.

A: Thank you so much.

B: You're welcome.

Listen

Listen to the conversation and check who can do the things in the chart.

	Type	Drive	Bake	Dance
Don				
Patrick				
Brenda				
Clara				

Pronunciation

Listen to the sentences and write either 'can' or 'can't' in the blanks.

1 Jane _____ speak a foreign language.
2 Kevin _____ play sports well.
3 I _____ tell you many interesting stories.
4 Marvin and Chris _____ swim, but they _____ dive.
5 My students _____ go on a picnic tomorrow.
6 Mr. Heather _____ drive well at night.

UNIT 09 Where was he last night?

Start

Where do people do these things? Match each activity with the place it is done.

- get a suntan
- go snowboarding
- read and relax
- hang out with friends
- run on the treadmill
- see a jazz concert
- get groceries
- look at old paintings

- at the shopping mall
- at the beach
- at the ski resort
- at the gym
- at the art center
- at the library
- at the supermarket
- at the museum

Dialogue

Listen to the dialogue and practice.

Scott: Janet, where were you last night? I called you, but the answering machine picked up.
Janet: I was at Pleasant Hill Shopping Mall.
Scott: Oh, what were you doing there?
Janet: I was looking around at Stacy's. They had a one-day sale.
Scott: Really! How was it?
Janet: It was very crowded. But I got a real bargain on a nice pair of shoes.
Scott: Wow, you were lucky.

Grammar | Simple past of be verb / Past progressive

Simple past of be verb

I / He / She **was** at home last night.
wasn't at home last night.

You / We / They **were** at home last night.
weren't friends in 1995.

Was Jake at the club yesterday? → Yes, he was. / No, he wasn't.
Were you in Paris in 1992? → Yes, I was. / No, I wasn't.
When was Nicole in China? → She was there in 2005.
Where were they last night? → They were at the beach.

Past progressive

I / He / She **was** sleeping.
wasn't sleeping.

You / We / They **were** sleeping.
weren't sleeping.

Was Carrie study**ing** last Sunday? → Yes, she was. / No, she wasn't.
Were they study**ing** last night? → Yes, they were. / No, they weren't.
What were you do**ing** last Sunday? → I was swimming at the beach.
What was Carrie do**ing** last Sunday? → She was studying.

Speak 1 | Where were they?

Complete the sentences with the correct past form of be verb.

1. Jake _____ at the gym.
2. Tim and Monica _____ at the library.
3. Cindy _____ at the movie theater.
4. Mr. Goodman _____ at the Charlie's Bar.
5. David _____ at the bookstore.
6. My sisters _____ at our grandmother's house.

Practice the dialogue using the information above.

A: Was Karen with you last night?
B: No, she wasn't.
A: Then where was she?
B: She was at Jake's party.

Where was he last night?

Speak 2 | How was it?

Practice the dialogue using the information below.

> A: **When** was Monica at the restaurant?
> B: She was there this morning.
> A: **How** was the food?
> B: It was very delicious.

① Jane and Austin were at the concert last night. The music was pleasant.
② Jennifer was at the beach this afternoon. The weather was great.
③ My uncle was at the gallery two days ago. The paintings were wonderful.
④ Micheal was at the movies yesterday. The movie was touching.
⑤ Sylvia and her sister were at the mall this morning. The shopping was fun.

Speak 3 | Giving alibis

A detective is talking to people about where they were and what they were doing at 10 last night. Work in pairs. One of you will be the detective, and the other will be one of the people below. Switch roles with your partner.

> A: **Where** were you last night?
> B: I was at the beach.
> A: **What** were you doing?
> B: I was walking along the beach.

1. Mark
   - at the library
   - study for the final exam

2. Dana
   - at the mall
   - shop for clothes

3. Brian
   - at the bar
   - drink beer

4. Amy
   - at home
   - watch TV

5. Peter
   - at the gym
   - work out

6. Mary
   - at an Internet cafe
   - surf the Web

Activity 1 | At the same time

 Step 1 Get into groups of four. First, write what you were doing at the times below. Then take turns saying what you were doing. Write down what your group members say.

e.g. I was having dinner with my family.

	You	#1	#2	#3
Last Saturday night				
At 9:00 last night				
At 7:00 this morning				

 Step 2 Take turns saying what you and the other members of your group were doing at the times above. Follow the example below.

e.g.
- **You (Jay):** I was seeing a concert last Saturday night.
- **#1 (Tom):** Last Saturday night, Jay was seeing a concert, and I was studying at the library.
- **#2 (Jack):** Last Saturday night, Tom was studying at the library, and I was hanging out with friends at the park.
- **#3 (Kelly):** Last Saturday night, Jack was hanging out with friends at the park, and I was buying groceries at the supermarket.

Activity 2 | Chris and Nicole in 1997

 Read about what Chris and Nicole were doing at different points of time in the past.

Chris

In 1997, I was 20 years old. I was living in Toronto with my parents. I was studying piano at college. Last year, I was teaching at a community college. I was working hard. It was an excellent job.

Last month, I was in Vienna on a business trip. I was playing the piano in three concerts. They were all fantastic.

Nicole

In 1997, I was 25 years old. I was studying fashion design in Paris. It was tough, but I was learning a lot.

Last year, I was working as a designer for a clothing company in New York. I really enjoyed the work. Last month, I was in Seoul. I was attending several fashion shows. They were very successful.

 With a partner, discuss the questions below.

Chris	Q1. Where was Chris in 1997, and what was he doing then?
	Q2. When was he teaching music? How was the job?
	Q3. Where was he last month? What was he doing there?
Nicole	Q1. Where was Nicole in 1997, and what was she doing then?
	Q2. When was she in New York? What was she doing there?
	Q3. What was she doing in Seoul? How were the shows?

Listen

Listen to the conversations and choose the correct answer to each question.

Conversation 1

Q1 Where was Karen last night?
 a at Peter's party
 b at home

Q2 Who was Karen with?
 a with her mother
 b with her boyfriend

Conversation 2

Q1 How was the movie?
 a fun
 b boring

Q2 Who was Jason with at the theater?
 a with Michelle
 b by himself

Conversation 3

Q1 When was Peter at the gym?
 a last night
 b last Sunday

Q2 What was he doing?
 a running on the treadmill
 b lifting weights

Pronunciation

Listen to the following sentences and circle the correct words.

1 Max (was, wasn't) having lunch with his wife.
2 Christina (was, wasn't) sleeping in her bed.
3 Maria and her husband (were, weren't) talking to the doctor.
4 My father (was, wasn't) enjoying the parade.
5 Last night, my parents (were, weren't) shopping at the mall.
6 Michelle (was, wasn't) enjoying the movie.
7 Many people (were, weren't) attending the concert.
8 Yesterday, I (was, wasn't) playing with my cousin.

UNIT 10 — What did you do yesterday?

Start

Look at the list of holidays and special days. What do you know about them?

Holidays and special days

- New Year's Day
- Valentine's Day
- Halloween
- Thanksgiving Day
- Christmas
- Birthday

What do people do on these days? Put the right day next to each activity.

1. People wear party hats and blow out candles on a cake.
2. Children go trick or treating from house to house.
3. People eat roast turkey with cranberry sauce.
4. People decorate their house with lights and give presents to each other.

Dialogue

Listen to the dialogue and practice.

Molly: Where were you yesterday? I called you three times!
Olivia: I was at the library. Why?
Molly: You know, tomorrow is Maria's birthday.
Olivia: Oh, I forgot!
Molly: That's ok. You still have one day left.
Olivia: What did you buy for her?
Molly: I bought some perfume.
Olivia: I'm sure she'll like it very much.

Grammar | Simple past: Regular and irregular verbs

Regular verb

- call → call**ed**
- like → lik**ed**
- *study → stud**ied**
- *stop → stop**ped**

Irregular verb (no specific rules)

- come → **came**
- make → **made**
- drive → **drove**
- put → **put**
- go → **went**
- write → **wrote**
- get → **got**
- cut → **cut**
- take → **took**
- eat → **ate**
- see → **saw**
- read → **read** [red]

He **came** to my house yesterday.
She **did not (didn't)** come to my house yesterday.

Did you see the baseball game?   *Yes, I did.* / *No, I didn't.*

Where did you go last night?	→ I went to Jane's wedding.
Who did you go with?	→ I went with my mom.
What did you do there?	→ I danced with the bride.
How did you get there?	→ I took the subway.
When did you get home?	→ I got home around 11.

Speak 1 | Did you enjoy it?

Practice the dialogue using the information below.

A: I **went** to a party last night.
B: **Did** you **enjoy** it?
A: Yes, I did. It was fantastic. / No, I didn't. It was awful.

Who	Where	When	How
I	a movie	yesterday	touching
Mary	a rock concert	last Saturday	exciting
Chris	an amusement park	last Sunday	fun
My parents	a basketball game	two days ago	boring
Pam & Peter	a night club	a week ago	too crowded

Speak 2 | Did or didn't

1 Complete the sentences with the proper past forms of the verbs in the box.

Yesterday,
- Kevin _____ to a concert.
- Robin _____ a movie on DVD.
- Steven _____ some friends over.
- Mr. Jones _____ late at the office.
- Jeremy and Kate _____ the kitchen.

Verb list

work paint invite
watch go

2 Make up dialogues by changing the highlighted parts with the expressions from the above.

> A: Did Ryan study yesterday?
> B: No, he didn't.
> A: What did he do then?
> B: He read a book.

Speak 3 | Holidays

Read the sentences first and practice the dialogue using the sentences below.

> A: Did you have a good time on Thanksgiving Day?
> B: Sure. I had fun.
> A: What did you do?
> B: I went on a trip with my family.
> A: Oh, where did you go?
> B: We went to Lake Tahoe.
> A: What did you do there?
> B: We stayed in a log house near the lake and relaxed.
> A: Sounds great.

❶ On Halloween, I visited my grandparents in Chicago. There, I went trick or treating with other children. We got a lot of candy.

❷ On My birthday, I went fishing on the west coast with my friends. We had a party there, and I blew out the candles on the cake.

❸ At Christmas, I took a trip to Yosemite with my family. We stayed at a log house, and I gave presents to my parents and brothers.

❹ On Thanksgiving Day, I went to my friend's house in LA. I ate roast turkey with cranberry sauce.

Activity 1 | Hot spots for the weekend

 Step 1 Three people are talking about some good places they visited over the weekend. Read their stories.

Hot Spots for Your Weekend!

Lotus Club

I went to Lotus Club on 5th Avenue last Friday, and it was awesome! People were dancing and drinking beer. My friend Erica loved it, too. The entrance fee is 10 dollars. Try Lotus Club. It's the hottest place in New York.

Michelle Williams

San Diego Zoo

Daniel Fisher

A zoo is not just for kids anymore! I went to the famous San Diego Zoo last weekend, and it was really fun! I saw many exotic animals and the dolphin show. Honestly, I didn't expect that much, but I really enjoyed it.

Museum of Modern Art

Amy Kwan

I went to MOMA, the Museum of Modern Art, with my boyfriend yesterday. I tried to go there twice before, but it was closed for renovations. I saw a lot of interesting paintings and sculptures there. It was very educational.

 Step 2 With a partner, talk about the following questions.

1 Who went to Lotus Club last Friday?
2 What did Daniel see at the San Diego Zoo?
3 When did Michelle go to the Lotus Club?
4 Who did Amy go to MOMA with?

 Step 3 Did you visit any interesting places over the weekend? Or can you think of any hot spots you visited before? With a partner, talk about the places you visited. Use the questions below.

- Where did you go?
- When did you go there?
- Who did you go with?
- What did you do there?

Activity 2 | Sending a postcard

 Step 1 Angela is traveling around Japan. She is writing a postcard to her friend, Sally. She is writing about what she did yesterday. Complete the postcard below using the past tense.

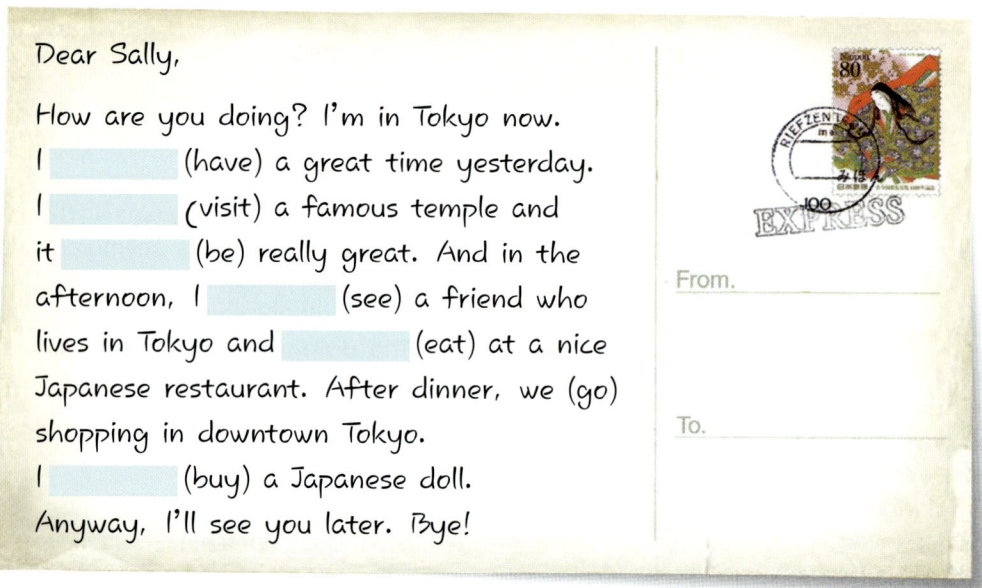

Dear Sally,

How are you doing? I'm in Tokyo now. I _____ (have) a great time yesterday. I _____ (visit) a famous temple and it _____ (be) really great. And in the afternoon, I _____ (see) a friend who lives in Tokyo and _____ (eat) at a nice Japanese restaurant. After dinner, we (go) shopping in downtown Tokyo. I _____ (buy) a Japanese doll. Anyway, I'll see you later. Bye!

 Step 2 Imagine that you are in a foreign country. Write a postcard to one of your friends about what you did last weekend. Use the past tense.

Listen

You will hear a short biography about Tiger Woods. Listen carefully and choose the correct answer for each question.

Q1 When was he born?
- a in 1975
- b in 1977
- c in 1978

Q2 When did he begin to play golf?
- a at age two
- b at age three
- c at age four

Q3 Which university did he go to?
- a UCLA
- b Berkeley
- c Stanford

Q4 How many games did he win on the PGA tour?
- a more than 43
- b more than 53
- c more than 63

Pronunciation

Listen to the following verbs and check (✓) the correct /d/, /t/ or /id/ ending sound.

	/d/	/t/	/id/
1 played			
2 wanted			
3 washed			
4 listened			
5 needed			
6 practiced			
7 shopped			
8 liked			

UNIT 11 How many apples do you need?

Start

Choose the proper word for each blank from the list.

A slice of ham
A cup of coffee
A carton of milk
A bag of flour

A box of chocolate
A piece of cake
A can of tuna
A bottle of wine

water   cheese   pizza   cereal
tea   coke   juice   sugar

Dialogue

Listen to the dialogue and practice.

Liz: Do you have any baking soda?
Dorothy: Yeah, I have some. Here you are.
Liz: Thanks. I'm going to make some apple pies.
Dorothy: For your son's birthday party?
Liz: Yes, his friends are coming over. Oh, I need some napkins, too.
Dorothy: There are many napkins in my cupboard. I'll lend you some.

Grammar | Countable and uncountable nouns

	Singular	Plural	
Countable Nouns	a banana	two bananas	A banana is on the table. There are two bananas.
Uncountable Nouns	milk	✗	Milk is good for your health.

Countable	Uncountable
many, a few, few	much, a little, little
some / any / a lot of	

many apples	much cheese
a few apples	a little cheese

I need **some** apples / cheese.
I don't need **any** apples / cheese.
Do you need **any** apples / cheese?

Speak 1 | Do you have any...?

Look at the pictures below and practice the dialogue with a partner.

A: I need **some** apples.
Do you have **any** apples?
B: Let me check.
Oh, there are **some** apples.
Here you are.

A: I need **some** ice.
Do you have **any** ice?
B: Let me check.
I'm sorry, there isn't **any** ice.

you have

you don't have

How many apples do you need? 69

Speak 2 | Is there enough milk?

Work with a partner. You are preparing for tonight's party. Check if you have enough of what you need.

A: Is there enough milk in the fridge?
B: No, there isn't.
There is only a little milk.

A: Are there enough forks on the table?
B: No, there aren't.
There are just a few forks.

Speak 3 | Grocery shopping

You are going grocery shopping. Talk with your partner about what you need to get. Use the items in the lists.

A: I'm going to the grocery store. Do you need anything?
B: Yes, I need some apples and some pie.
A: How many apples do you need?
B: Five apples.
A: And how much pie?
B: Three pieces.
A: Anything else?
B: No, that's all.

Things to buy
three tomatoes
three pounds of beef

Things to buy
two onions
one carton of milk

Things to buy
four lemons
one box of cereal

70 UNIT 11

Activity 1 | They are good for your health

 Step 1 Studies show that these foods are good for your health. Which of these foods do you like to eat? Make the list of the foods you usually like to eat.

apples almonds broccoli sweet potatoes garlic

tomatoes red beans kiwis salmon spinach

Foods I like to eat...

 Step 2 Write about what foods you like to eat and how much (many) of it (them) you have every day or every week.

Example

I like to eat tomatoes. I eat one tomato every day.
I like to eat garlic. I eat some garlic bread every day.
I like to eat salmon. I eat some salmon every week.

 Step 3 With a partner, talk about what foods you like to eat and how much (many) of it (them) you have based on the sentences above.

Questions

What foods do you like to eat?
How much _____ do you eat every day?
How many _____ do you eat every week?

How many apples do you need? 71

Activity 2 | Recipe

Step 1 Kelly and Jasmine are going to make chicken sandwiches together. Go through the recipe.

Step 2 With your partner, complete the dialogue below based on the information above. Then, practice the dialogue.

Kelly: I'm starving.
Jasmine: Me, too. How about having _____ chicken sandwiches?
Kelly: Sounds yummy. Do you know how to make them?
Jasmine: Sure, it's easy.
Kelly: Alright. Do we have everything we need to make them?
Jasmine: Let's check the refrigerator.
Kelly: Hmm, we have some _____. How much do we need of it?
Jasmine: We need _____.
Kelly: Then we have enough of it.
Jasmine: Here, we have _____.
Kelly: OK. We also have _____ and _____.
Jasmine: We don't have any _____ and _____.
Kelly: Oh, I'll go get _____ from the grocery store.
Jasmine: OK, I'll get the other ingredients ready.

Listen

Cathy and Mark had dinner at a fancy restaurant yesterday. Listen to the recording and write **C** for the food that Cathy had and **M** for the food that Mark had.

C / M	Food
	seafood pasta
	broccoli soup
	apple pie
	chocolate brownie
	pineapple juice
	New York steak
	garden salad
	iced tea

Listen again and write the appropriate quantifier for each menu item.

	broccoli soup
	apple pie
	pineapple juice

Pronunciation

You will hear one of the words in each of the following pairs. Listen and circle the word you hear.

1	pin	fin	5	leap	leaf
2	pill	fill	6	stripe	strife
3	peel	feel	7	copy	coffee
4	pan	fan	8	snip	sniff

How many apples do you need? 73

UNIT 12 I'd like to go rollerblading

Start

Here are some activities you can do in your free time. Which of them do you like to do? Which don't you like to do?

Free time activities
- read books
- go shopping
- get some rest
- cook special foods
- listen to music
- play computer games
- watch TV
- go for a drive
- go to the movies
- hang out with friends
- do exercises
- surf the Web

I like to...

I don't like to...

Dialogue

Listen to the dialogue and practice.

Andy: What do you like to do in your free time?
Mike: I like to go rollerblading.
Andy: Oh, I want to go rollerblading, too.
Mike: Then, would you like to join us this Saturday? I'm going rollerblading with my friends at Riverside Park.
Andy: Sure, I'd like that. Where do you want me to meet you?
Mike: Come to the parking lot in front of the park by 9:30.
Andy: Okay. I'll see you then.

Grammar | Gerund / Infinitive

What do you like to do in your free time?

I like to watch TV.
I like watching TV.

want + to V

I (don't) want to help her.
Do you want to help her?

What do you want to do?
→ I want to help her.

want + someone + to V

I (don't) want him to help her.
Do you want him to help her?

What do you want him to do?
→ I want him to help her.

- Would you like to go to a movie on Sunday?
  (= Do you want to go to a movie on Sunday?)

  Yes, I'd like to.
  I'd like to, but I have to study.

- What would you like to do on Sunday?
  (= What do you want to do on Sunday?)

  I'd like to go to a movie.

Speak 1 | In your free time

Practice the dialogue using the words below.

A: What do you like to do in your free time?
B: I like to play sports.
A: What kind of **sports** do you like playing?
B: I like **playing soccer**.

play sports	>	soccer · basketball · tennis
listen to music	>	rock · classical music · pop
watch movies	>	comedies · horror · sci-fi
read books	>	novels · mysteries · poems

Speak 2 | I want to...

You are talking to your friend about what you want to do this Saturday.

1 Match each expression on the left with the related expression on the right.

I want to...
- do housework
- have a barbeque
- study for the final exam
- go grocery shopping
- move to a new place

I want you to...
- get some sodas from the market
- carry the grocery bags
- clean the bathroom
- lend me your pick-up truck
- help me with my English

2 Talk with your partner about the above. Follow the example.

> A: What do you want to do this Saturday?
> B: I want to invite some friends over.
> A: Do you want me to help you?
> B: Sure. I want you to bake cookies.
> A: No problem.

Speak 3 | I'd like to, but...

Go over the expressions in the two boxes below. With your partner, make dialogues using the expressions. Follow the example.

Would you like to...?
- go on a picnic
- go hiking
- go for a bike ride
- go swimming
- go dancing

I'd like to, but I have to...
- work on the report
- visit a friend in the hospital
- baby-sit my little sister
- go on a business trip
- clean the garage

> A: Do you like going to concerts?
> B: Oh, I love it.
> A: Then would you like to go to a rock concert this Sunday?
> B: I'd like to, but I have to finish my term paper.
> A: I'm sorry to hear that. Let's get together some other time.
> B: Sure.

Activity 1 | Likes and dislikes

 Step 1 Two people are talking about what they like to do and don't like to do. Read their stories.

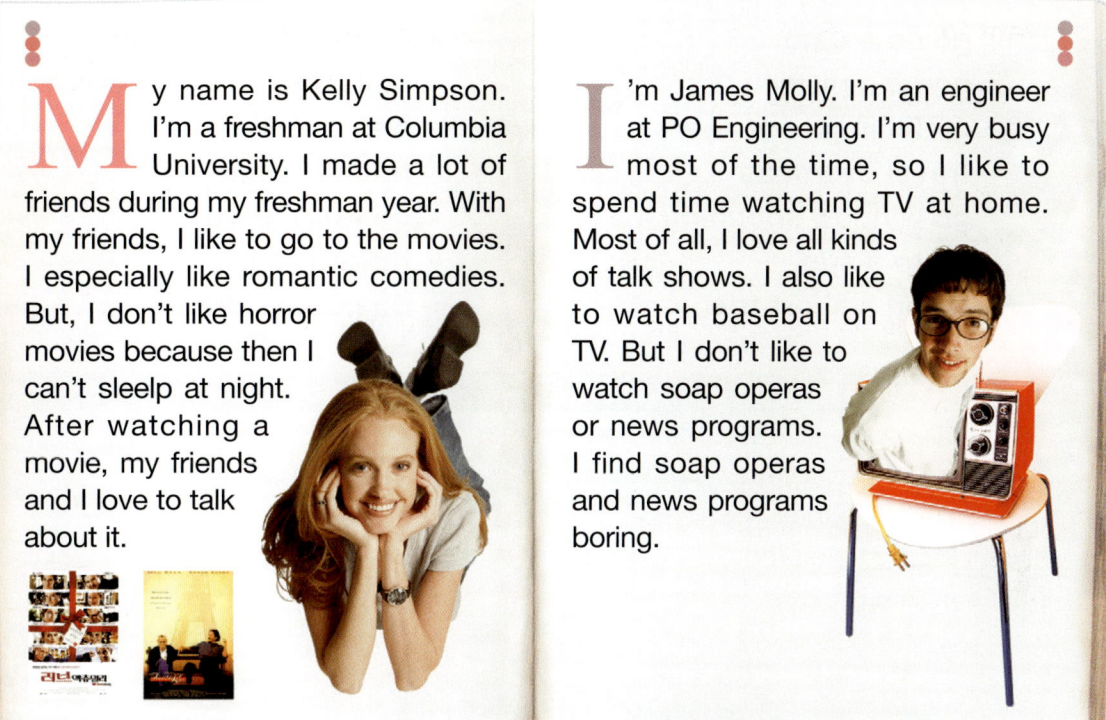

My name is Kelly Simpson. I'm a freshman at Columbia University. I made a lot of friends during my freshman year. With my friends, I like to go to the movies. I especially like romantic comedies. But, I don't like horror movies because then I can't sleelp at night. After watching a movie, my friends and I love to talk about it.

I'm James Molly. I'm an engineer at PO Engineering. I'm very busy most of the time, so I like to spend time watching TV at home. Most of all, I love all kinds of talk shows. I also like to watch baseball on TV. But I don't like to watch soap operas or news programs. I find soap operas and news programs boring.

 Step 2 Work with a partner. Talk about the following questions.

> What kinds of movies does Kelly like?
> Why doesn't Kelly like to see horror movies?
> What do Kelly and her friends like to do after watching movies?
>
> How about you? Talk about the kinds of movies you like / don't like.

> What kinds of TV programs does James like to watch?
> Why doesn't James like to watch soap operas and news programs?
>
> How about you? Talk about the TV programs you like / don't like.

I'd like to go rollerblading

Activity 2 | What would you like to do?

 Here are some things people like to do on the weekend or during vacation. Check the things you'd like to do on the weekend with a (#) and check the things you'd like to do during vacation with a (*). Then complete the chart below.

- go on a date
- go on a picnic
- go fishing
- travel overseas
- go window shopping
- go to a spa
- go on a short trip
- hang out with friends
- go hiking
- play sports
- relax at home
- go for a drive
- throw a party
- do housework

I'd like to ... on the weekend.	I'd like to ... during my vacation.

 With your partner, talk about the things you'd like to do this weekend and on your next vacation. See the example below.

Example

A: What would you like to do this weekend?
B: I'd like to go for a drive.
A: Sounds fun. Who would you like to go with?
B: I'd like to go with my boyfriend.
A: Where would you like to go?
B: I'd like to go to the beach. How about you? What would you like to do?
A: I'd like to sleep all day long.

Listen

Listen to the conversations and check (✓) whether the statements are true or false.

Conversation		True	False
1	Greg doesn't like to go to the zoo.		
2	Jack would like to go on a vacation to the beach.		
3	Michelle will spend time with her family on her day off.		
4	Mark wants his friend to help him this Saturday.		

Pronunciation

Listen to the following sentences and fill in the blanks with the words you hear.

1 I _____ become a famous physician when I grow up.
2 I'm _____ visit my grandmother's house this Saturday.
3 Don't worry. He's _____ pay the bill.
4 They _____ spend their vacation in Santa Monica this summer.
5 Jennifer loves traveling. She's _____ travel around France.
6 Kevin, is this what you _____ have?

UNIT 13 — He's tall and funny

Start

1 Study the words you can use when you describe things.

Color	Pattern	Shape
navy	checked	round / oval
purple	plaid	square
tan	solid	rectangular
yellow	polka dot	flat
gray	striped	long / short
brown	flowered	thick / thin

2 What words from the list can you use to describe each item below?

Dialogue

Listen to the dialogue and practice.

Mary: Kathy's new boyfriend was at the party yesterday.
Pam: Oh, really? I'd like to meet him someday. What's he like?
Mary: Well, he's very friendly and funny.
Pam: Is he cute? Kathy likes good-looking guys.
Mary: Not really.
Pam: Then what does he look like?
Mary: He's pretty short and chubby with long wavy hair.
Pam: Oh, that's very surprising.
Mary: You can say that again.

Grammar | Describing people and things

Describing a person: personality and appearance

What is he like?	He is honest / funny / smart / friendly.
What does he look like?	He is tall / medium-height / short.
	He is skinny / slim / average build / overweight.
	He has short, wavy and brown hair.
	He has medium-length, straight and black hair.
What is he wearing?	He is wearing a white shirt and a navy suit.
	He is wearing a green sweater and gray pants.

Describing things

What is the bag like?	It's square and brown.
What does the bag look like?	It's a square and brown bag.

Speak 1 | Newcomers

You didn't come to class for a week, and you found that there are some newcomers in your class. Talk to your partner about what they are like.

A: Who is that guy over there?
B: That is Rick.
A: He looks nice. What is he like?
B: Well, he's very active and kind.

Chris	Pamela	Todd	Amy
shy and serious	talkative and funny	brave and smart	friendly and cheerful

He's tall and funny

Speak 2 | At a garden party

You are at a garden party and talking to your friend about who their boyfriend / girlfriend is. Follow the example and use the words you learned in the Grammar section.

A: Is your girlfriend here?
B: Uh-huh, she's standing next to the table.
A: Which one is she? What does she look like?
B: She's tall and slim and has short, blonde hair. She's wearing a pink dress.
A: Oh, there she is.

Speak 3 | I can't find my sneakers

You're looking for some of your stuff. Talk to your partner about what they look like and find out where they are.

A: I can't find my sneakers.
B: What do they look like?
A: They are black with purple shoelaces.
B: Are these your sneakers?
A: Oh, there they are. Thanks.

I can't find my...

Activity 1 | What is your ideal type?

 Step 1 Two people are describing what their ideal type of a man / woman is. Read their stories.

Nicole

My ideal type of a man is pretty complex. I'm 28 years old, so I want him to be around 30, not younger than me. I'm a fashion designer, so I'd like to date a man working in the same industry. Also, he must be very tall since I'm rather tall. Finally, he needs to have good sense of humor. Is there any guy like this?

Jason

I'm 32 years old, and I'm an engineer. I'm quite busy with work, but I'd like to meet a perfect match. First, I want her to be around my age. And I like small women. What she does is not important, but I really care about personality. She should be very outgoing and active.

 Step 2 Talk about the following questions with a partner.

1 What is Nicole's ideal man like?
2 What is Jason's ideal woman like?

 Step 3 What's your ideal type? Talk about what he / she is like.

He's tall and funny

Activity 2 | At the gallery

 Step 1 Look at the picture very carefully. What do the things look like? What do the people look like? Try to describe the picture by completing the sentences below.

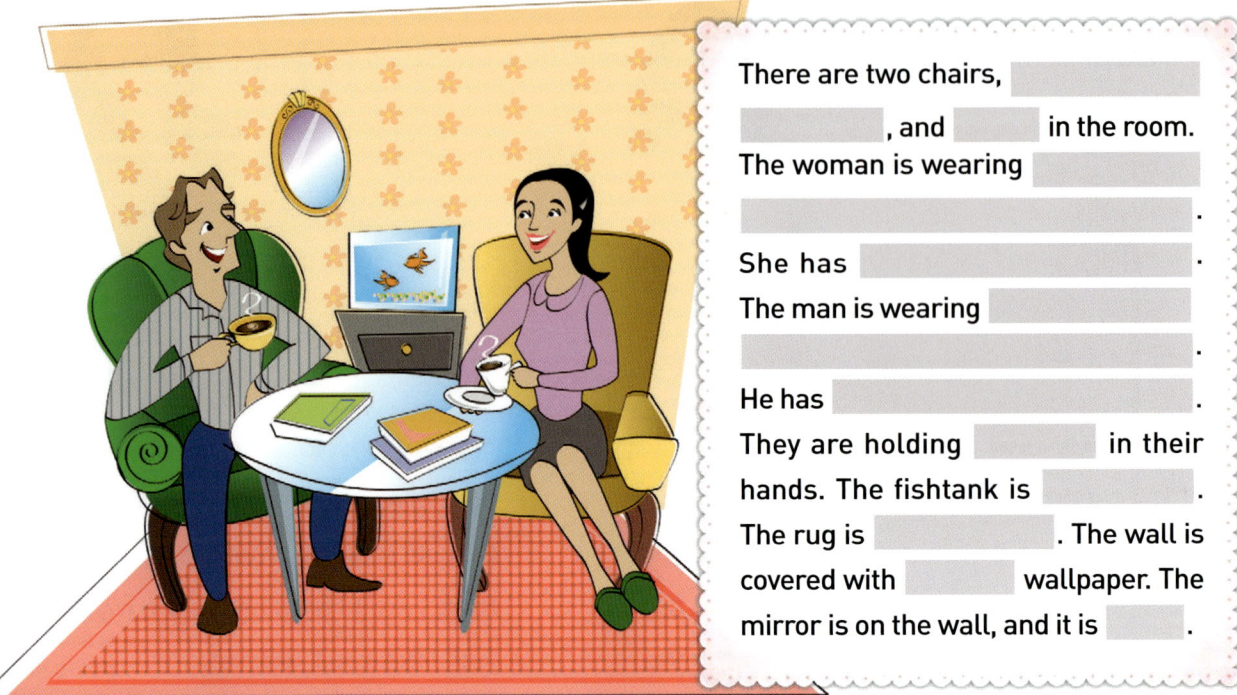

There are two chairs, _____, _____, and _____ in the room.
The woman is wearing _____ _____.
She has _____.
The man is wearing _____ _____.
He has _____.
They are holding _____ in their hands. The fishtank is _____.
The rug is _____. The wall is covered with _____ wallpaper. The mirror is on the wall, and it is _____.

 Step 2 First, draw a picture including people and a couple of objects like the one above. Then describe the picture to your partner. Your partner draws a picture while listening to your description. Finally, compare the two pictures.

Listen

Listen to the conversations and circle the answer to each question.

Conversation 1

Q What does the woman's dress look like? Circle the correct picture of the dress.

a    b    c

Conversation 2

Q Which of the following words cannot be used to describe the man's car?

a black   b medium-sized   c used

Conversation 3

Q Circle all the words that correctly describe the man Alice met.

| tall | kind | blue eyes | blond hair |
| funny | smart | brown eyes | dark brown hair |

Pronunciation

Listen to the following sentences and fill in the blanks with the words you hear.

1 Would you like some coffee _____ tea?
2 Did you say both pink _____ yellow T-shirts?
3 Will it be cash _____ charge?
4 Is it cheap _____ useful?
5 Do you want diet _____ regular Coke?
6 Do you have a driver's license _____ other identification?
7 I'd like to have fish _____ chips, please.
8 Is it for here _____ to go?

UNIT 14 — I go jogging every day

Start

How often do you do the things below? Check the appropriate box.

	always	usually	sometimes	rarely	never
get up before six					
have breakfast					
go jogging in the morning					
skip lunch					
drink coffee at night					
work late					
go hiking on the weekend					
go to bed early					

Dialogue

Listen to the dialogue and practice.

Danny: Do you often go out for dinner?

Brenda: Yeah, I don't like to cook. So, I usually go out for dinner.

Danny: What about weekends? Do you ever cook on weekends?

Brenda: Sometimes I cook dinner on Saturday. How about you? How often do you go out for dinner?

Danny: Once a week, only on Sunday. For the rest of the week, I have dinner at home.

Brenda: You must enjoy cooking!

Grammar | Adverbs of frequency

Do you drink coffee in the morning?

Yes,	I **always** drink coffee in the morning. **usually** **often** **sometimes**
No,	I **rarely** drink coffee in the morning. **never**

100%

0%

Frequency expressions

How often do you go to the movies? → I go to the movies once a week / twice a month.

How many times a week do you go jogging? → I go jogging three times a week.

Speak 1 | Who is healthy?

1 With a partner, talk about how often the people do these things.

	Drink coffee	Drive to work	Eat breakfast	Do exercises
1 Henry	never	always	often	never
2 Janet	sometimes	often	rarely	always
3 Todd	always	sometimes	never	never
4 Amy	rarely	never	always	often
5 Yourself				

A: Does Henry drink coffee?
B: No, he never drinks coffee.
A: How about Todd? Does he drink coffee?
B: Yes, he always drinks coffee.

---

2 Who do you think has a healthy lifestyle?

Speak 2 | Lifestyle

With a partner, talk about the people's lifestyles using the information given. Follow the example.

1. Mathew gets a medical check-up twice a year.
2. Kevin rarely goes out for a drink.
3. Maggie goes hiking every Sunday.
4. Elly never eats fast food.
5. Jamie goes for a walk five times a week.

> A: Does Greg ever go jogging?
> B: Yes, he does.
> A: How often does he go jogging?
> B: He goes jogging at least three times a week.
> A: Wow, three times a week? He must be healthy.

Speak 3 | Pastimes

With your partner, take turns being each of the people below. Talk about what you like to do and how often you do it. Follow the example.

 I like to bake cookies almost three times a week.

 I like to build model cars four times a week.

 I like to go window shopping every other day.

 I like to blog every day.

> A: I like to watch movies on TV.
> B: How many times a week do you watch movies on TV?
> A: Almost five times a week.
> B: Oh! You're really into it.
> A: Yes, I am.

Activity 1 | Jane's monthly schedule

Step 1 This calendar shows Jane's monthly schedule. With a partner, talk about her schedule by asking questions.

 visit her parents

 see her boyfriend

 take piano lessons

 play tennis

 go to church

 go shopping

Example questions

Q: How many times a week does Jane see her boyfriend?
Q: How often does Jane take piano lessons?

Step 2 Make a schedule that shows your monthly routines like the one above. Then with a partner, talk about your monthly routines.

Example

A: How often do you play computer games?
B: About four times a week. How about you?
A: I rarely play computer games.

I go jogging every day

Activity 2 | To live for 100 years

 Step 1 Sandy and Paul worry about their health. They want to live for a long time. Read their stories about their habits and find out what they do to stay healthy.

I'm Sandy, and I'm a high school math teacher. I want to live to be more than 100 years old. So, I always try to eat healthy food and get more exercise. I usually get up before six and have breakfast. I eat one apple and one tomato every day. I also go for a walk at least four times a week. Every Sunday, I go hiking in the mountains near my place. Sometimes, I go for a bike ride.

My name is Paul, and I'm a professional soccer player. For me, health is more important than anything else. That's why I never smoke. I always try to eat organic food and avoid junk food. Also, I usually go to bed before 11:00 and get up before 7:00. Sometimes, I go for a drink with buddies, but I usually drink just a little. I rarely drink coffee, and I take three kinds of vitamins every day.

 Step 2 Write sentences about what Sandy and Paul do to stay healthy.

Sandy always ....
She ....
She sometimes ....

Paul never .... and he ....
He usually ....
He ....

 Step 3 What do you do to stay healthy? Write about what you do to stay in shape.

Example

I usually get up early and go to bed early.

I never drink coffee or eat fast food.

I take a walk in the park every day.

I always eat a lot of vegetables.

Listen

Listen to the four conversations and check (✓) the correct box.

	Always	Sometimes	Never
1 Tom plays golf these days.			
2 Julie practices bowling.			
3 Peter drinks espresso.			
4 Kelly smokes.			

Pronunciation

Listen to the following sentences and circle the stressed words.

> **e.g.**   He (sometimes) goes (running) in the park.

1 How often do you go to the movies?
2 How many times a week do you work late?
3 She never goes out for drinks.
4 Jasmine goes to the movies twice a week.
5 I saw a movie last night with my girlfriend.
6 Can you help me with my homework?
7 This watch can tell you the date.
8 What does he look like?

UNIT 15 What are you going to do tonight?

Start

Do you have any plans for this weekend or any special plans for you next vacation? What are you going to do?

On the weekend
- get some rest
- study
- go shopping
- go to the movies
- do housework
- eat out
- have fun with friends

During the vacation
- take a short trip
- stay home and relax
- visit hometown
- read
- play sports
- clean the house
- travel abroad

What else are you going to do this weekend or during the vacation?

Dialogue

Listen to the dialogue and practice.

Tina: T. G. I. F.!
Ben: Yeah, it was a busy week.
Tina: What are you going to do this weekend?
Ben: I'm not sure. I guess I'll just stay home. How about you?
Tina: I'm going to throw a housewarming party on Sunday.
Ben: Oh, great!
Tina: Can you come? Actually, my friend Ally is coming.
Ben: Really? Then I'll be there for sure.

Grammar | Simple future: Be going to / Be ~ing / Will

Be going to

I'm (not) going to study English tonight.
Are you going to study English tonight?
→ Yes, I am. / No, I'm not.

What are you going to do tonight?
→ I'm going to study English.

Be ~ing

I'm (not) studying English tonight.
Are you studying English tonight?
→ Yes, I am. / No, I'm not.

What are you doing tonight?
→ I'm studying English.

Will

I will (won't) call you tonight.
→ Will you call me tonight?
→ Yes, I will. / No, I won't.

When will you call me tonight?
→ I'll call you around eight.

Be going to (plans already made)	Will (possible plans)
What are you going to do this weekend?	
• I'm going to go camping. • I'm going to go hiking.	• I'll just stay home. • Maybe I'll watch some DVDs.

Speak 1 | Weekend schedule

With your partner, talk about what you're going to do this weekend. Use the expressions below.

A: What are you going to do this weekend?
B: I'm going to go rollerblading. How about you?
A: I'm going to see my friend.
B: Sounds great. Have fun.

- go on a blind date
- relax at home
- go on a picnic
- go to the amusement park
- go shopping for clothes
- do some housework

Speak 2 | Future plans

Go over the information about the people's plans. Then with your partner, talk about their plans. Follow the example.

- This Friday, Janet is going camping to Redwood Park for two days.
- This winter, Gary is going skiing at Deer Valley Resort for three days.
- On his next vacation, Pete is going on a trip to Thailand for five days.
- Next week, Lisa is going to visit her uncle in Italy for a week.
- This summer, Jason is going to teach English at an English camp for three weeks.

A: What is Tom going to do this summer?
B: He's going to work part time.
A: Oh, where is he going to work?
B: At Joe's grocery.
A: For how long?
B: Three weeks.

Speak 3 | Maybe I'll...

Talk about plans for a holiday with your partner. Use the expressions below.

A: Do you have any plans for the holiday?
B: Not yet. Maybe I'll just spend time with my family.
A: I'm going to see a rock concert. Why not come with me? It'll be fun!
B: A rock concert! Okay, I'll go with you.

Maybe I'll...
walk my dog
go grocery shopping
do some housework
watch some DVDs
fix my bicycle
take my car to the garage

Why not...?
go skating
go to a soccer game
go fishing at the lake
see the motor show
go to a barbecue
see the fireworks at the park

94 UNIT 15

Activity 1 | What a vacation!

 Pam and Monica are going on a vacation to Hawaii for three days. Pam made all the plans. Read Pam's vacation plans below.

Plans for the trip to Hawaii

- ☐ Dates: from April 1st to April 3rd
- ☐ Airfare: $450
- ☐ Airline: United Airlines
- ☐ Hotel: The Marriott
- ☐ Hotel rate: $150

Things to do

Day 1 — APRIL 1st
- visit Kawai Island and caves
- get massages

Day 2 — APRIL 2nd
- go shopping
- go sailing at Waikiki Beach

Day 3 — APRIL 3rd
- snorkeling
- see Hawaiian folk dancing with Pam's friends

 Make up questions about the trip and what they are going to do on their vacation. Then with your partner, take turns asking and answering the questions.

1. When _____ they _____? (leave for Hawaii)
2. How _____? (get there)
3. Where _____? (stay)
4. How much _____? (pay for the room)
5. How long _____? (stay there)
6. What _____ on the first day?
7. Where _____ on the second day?
8. Who _____ on the third day?

Activity 2 | Writing an email

 Step 1 Read Alex's email to his friend, Anne.

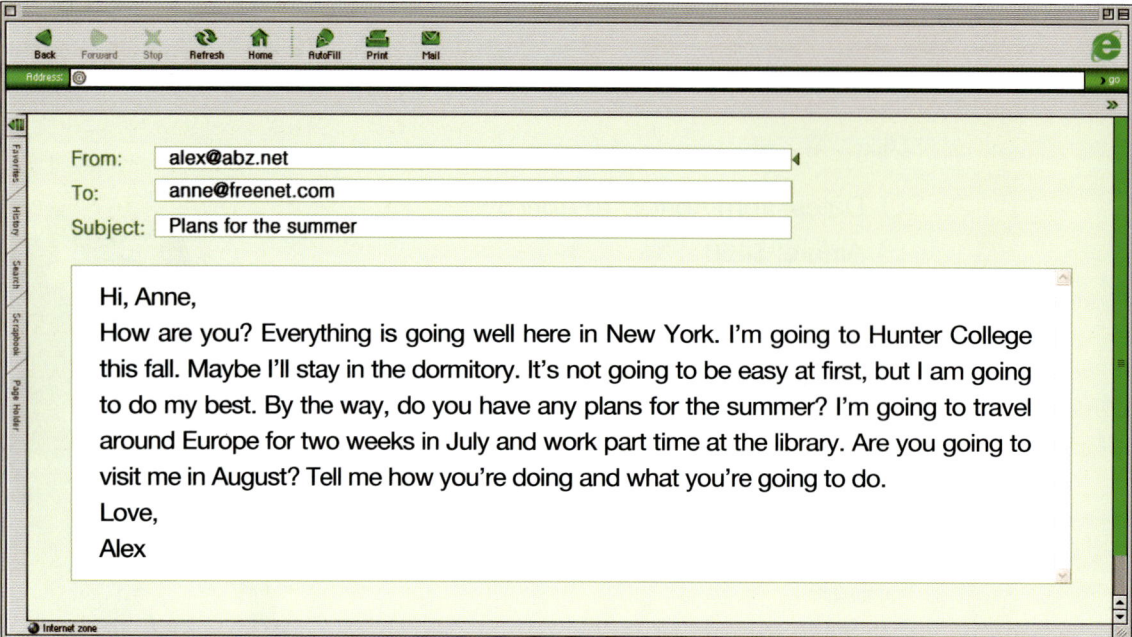

From: alex@abz.net
To: anne@freenet.com
Subject: Plans for the summer

Hi, Anne,
How are you? Everything is going well here in New York. I'm going to Hunter College this fall. Maybe I'll stay in the dormitory. It's not going to be easy at first, but I am going to do my best. By the way, do you have any plans for the summer? I'm going to travel around Europe for two weeks in July and work part time at the library. Are you going to visit me in August? Tell me how you're doing and what you're going to do.
Love,
Alex

 Step 2 Pretend you are Alex's friend, Anne. Complete the reply to his email below.

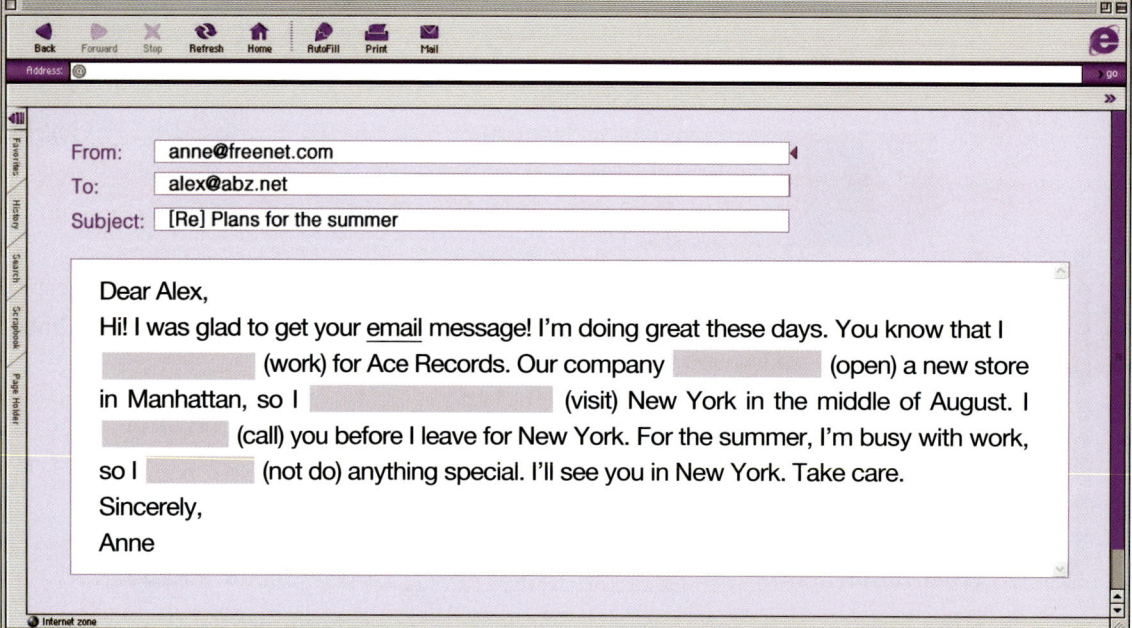

From: anne@freenet.com
To: alex@abz.net
Subject: [Re] Plans for the summer

Dear Alex,
Hi! I was glad to get your email message! I'm doing great these days. You know that I _____ (work) for Ace Records. Our company _____ (open) a new store in Manhattan, so I _____ (visit) New York in the middle of August. I _____ (call) you before I leave for New York. For the summer, I'm busy with work, so I _____ (not do) anything special. I'll see you in New York. Take care.
Sincerely,
Anne

 Step 3 Try to write your own email to your friend about your plans for your next vacation.

Listen

A. Charles is talking to Michael about the housewarming party at his place. Listen to the conversation and answer the following questions.

Q1 When is the party?

It's _____ .

Q2 What are the people going to have for dinner?

They are going to _____ .

Q3 What is Charles going to make for the guests?

He _____ .

B. Mandy is talking to Christine about her blind date yesterday. Listen to the conversation and check (✓) whether each sentence is true or false.

		True	False
1	Mandy is going to see the guy again.		
2	She will call him tonight.		
3	Maybe she will meet him this Sunday.		

Pronunciation

You will hear one of the words in each of the following pairs. Listen and circle the word you hear.

1	fly	fry	5	play	pray
2	liver	river	6	glass	grass
3	lock	rock	7	cloud	crowd
4	light	right	8	long	wrong

UNIT 16 Could you tell me how to get there?

Start

Where are the shops and places located in the map? Complete the sentences below by filling in the blanks with proper prepositions from the box.

across from
in front of
behind
next to / beside
between A and B

1 There is a drugstore _____ the post office.
2 The bank is _____ the post office.
3 The bakery is _____ the supermarket _____ the drug store.
4 There is a beauty salon _____ the bakery.
5 The bus stop is _____ the supermarket.

Dialogue

Listen to the dialogue and practice.

Ken: Excuse me, ma'am. Is there a hardware store around here?
Grace: Yeah, there's one near the shopping mall.
Ken: I'm new to the area. Could you tell me how to get there?
Grace: Sure. Walk up this street for two blocks and turn right. You'll see the shopping mall on the left. It's next to the mall.
Ken: Got it. Thanks a lot.
Grace: Sure.

Grammar | Locations and directions

Asking about and describing locations

Question	Response
• Is there a bakery around here? • Where is the bakery?	• It's across from the coffee shop. • It's next to the post office. • It's between the restaurant and the bookstore. • It's on Broadway.

Asking for and giving directions

Question	Response
• How can I get to the library? • Could you tell me how to get to the library?	• Go straight up this street for two blocks. • Turn left / right (at the corner). • It's on the left / right.

Speak 1 | Locations of places

You are new in town. With your partner, take turns asking about and describing the locations of some places around town.

A: Is there a music store around here?
B: Yes, there is one next to the hospital.
A: And where is the gift shop?
B: It's across from the parking garage.

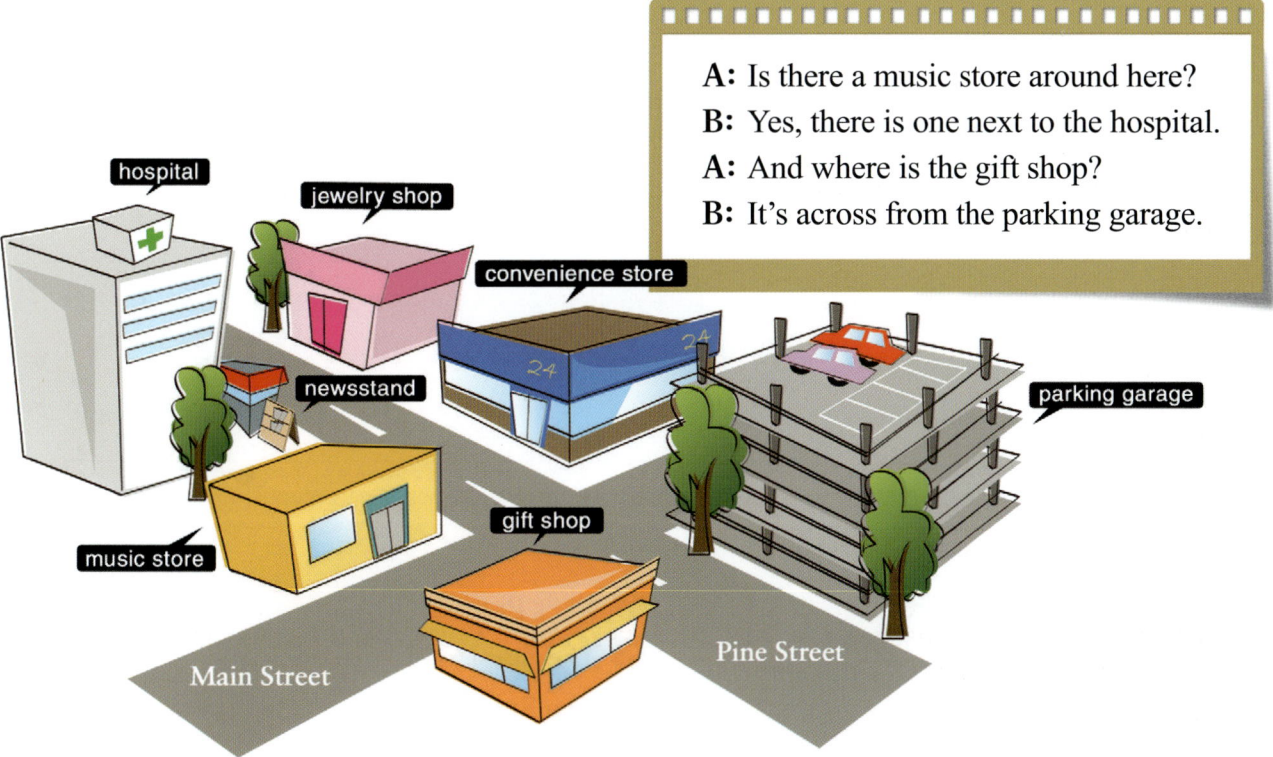

Speak 2 | How can I get to the bank?

Below is a map of the downtown area of a city. With a partner, take turns asking and answering questions about how to get to the places in the picture.

A: Excuse me. How can I get to City Hall?
B: City Hall? Walk up Broadway to Bank Street and turn right. It's on the left.
A: Thanks a lot.
B: No problem.

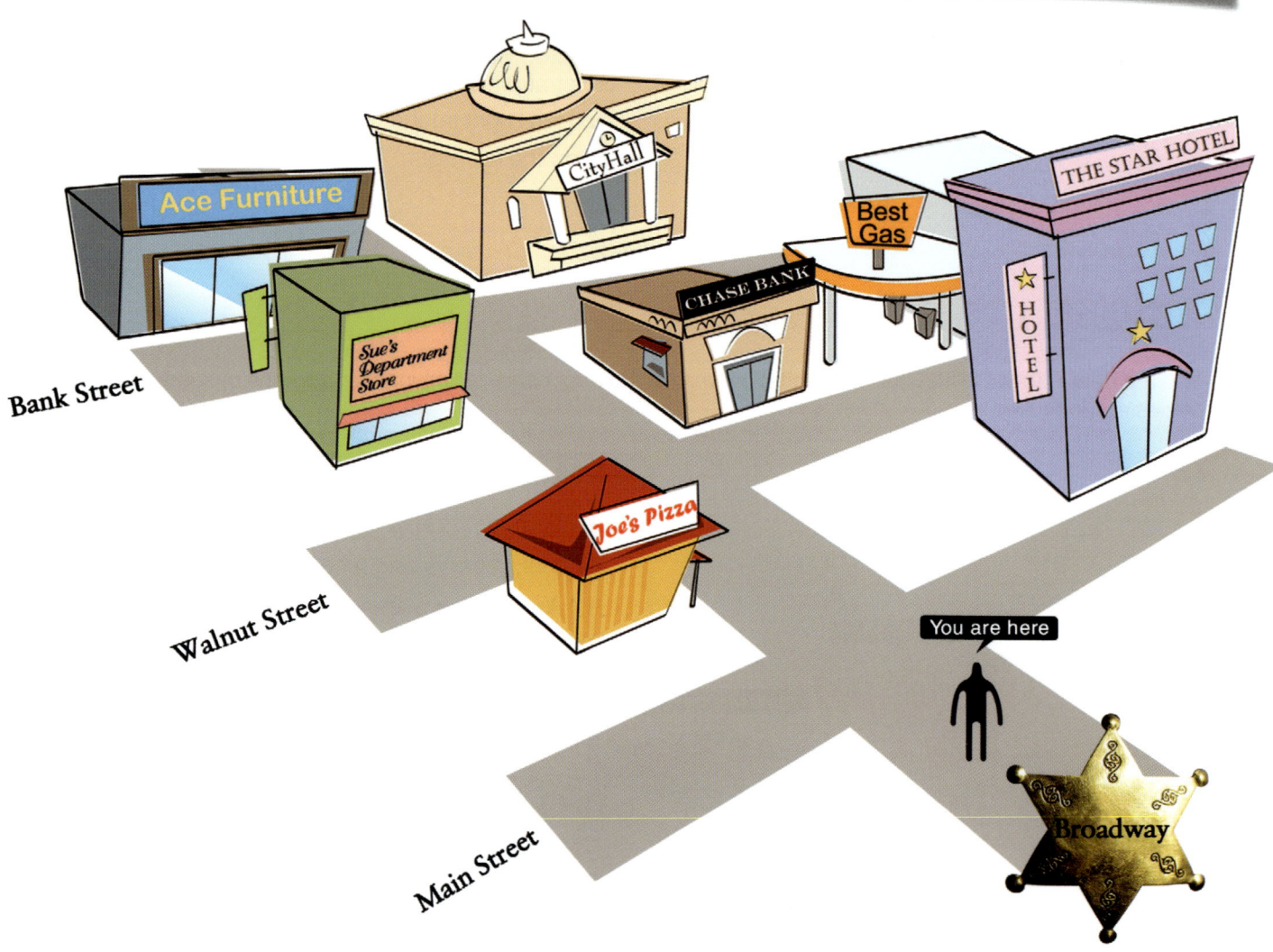

1. Sue's Department Store
2. Chase Bank
3. Best Gas Station
4. Joe's Pizza
5. The Star Hotel
6. Ace Furniture

Activity 1 | The way around the campus

 Step 1 Michelle is a freshman at the university. She does not know how to get around the campus, so she is asking her friend Charles where the places are located. Look at the map and complete the dialogue.

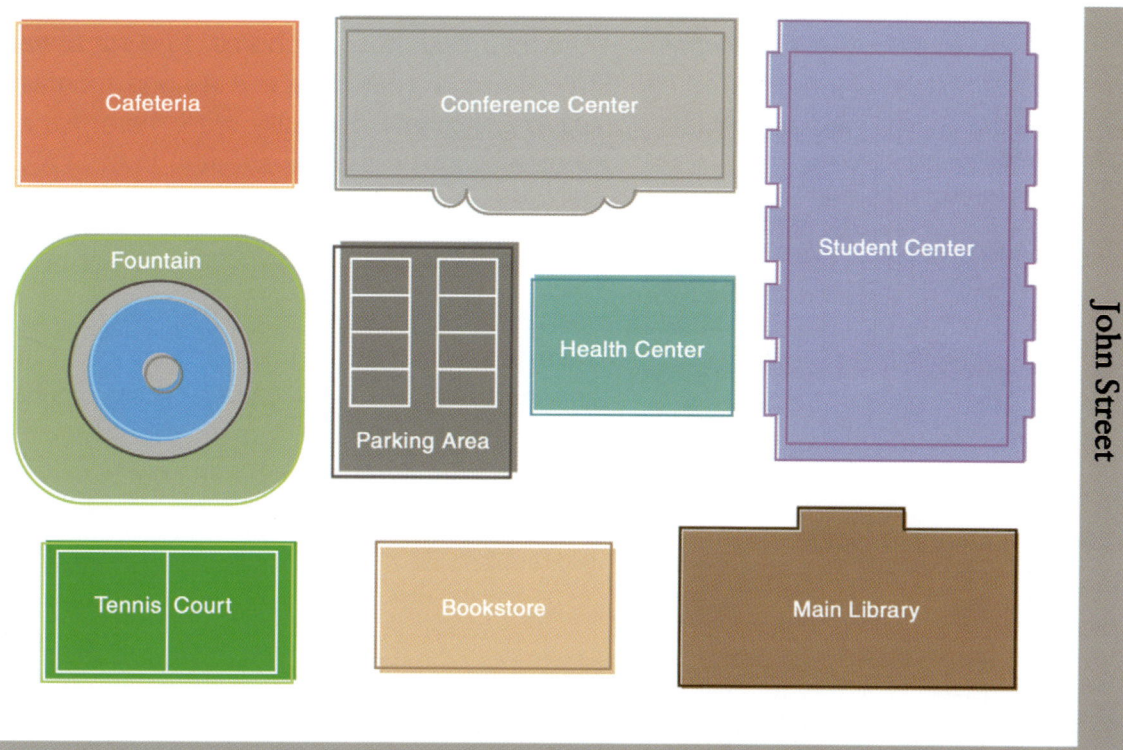

Michelle: Charles, do you know where the student center is?
Charles: Yeah, it's _____ the main library.
Michelle: Where's the main library, by the way?
Charles: It's _____ Maple Street and John Street.
Michelle: Oh, I see. So, where's the conference center?
Charles: It's _____ the cafeteria and student center.
Michelle: How about the _____?
Charles: Well, it's located between the tennis court and the main library.
Michelle: Wow, it's hard to get around.
Charles: You'll get used to it after a while.

 Step 2 Draw a map showing where the places are located around your home, school, or workplace. With your partner, make up a dialogue about the locations of the places like the one above.

Could you tell me how to get there? 101

Activity 2 | My favorite places

 People are talking about how to get to the places they often visit near their home, school, or workplace. Read the passages.

 There is a park near my home. I go for a walk there three times a week. There is a huge fountain and a nice walking path. I usually walk there. It's only five minutes away. I cross the street in front of my house, turn right, and go straight ahead. It's on the corner of Apple Street and Park Avenue.

 There is an Internet cafe near my school. I often go there and play computer games. There is a big street in front of the school. I go up the street for three blocks to Orinda Square and turn right. It's on the right, next to the Civic Library.

 There is a good Chiness restaurant near the company where I work. I often have dinner there with my coworkers. There is a subway station in front of the company building. I cross the street through the station. Then I walk up Central Road for about five minutes and turn right at 2nd Street. It's between the post office and Lily's Flower Shop.

 Choose one of the places you often visit near your home, school, or workplace. Then write the directions to that place. Use the proper expressions or words from the readings above.

How to get to _____ **from my** _____

There is ....

I ....

....

It's ....

Listen

Where do you want to go in SOHO? Now you are on the corner of Greene street and Spring Street. Listen to the directions and number the places on the map.

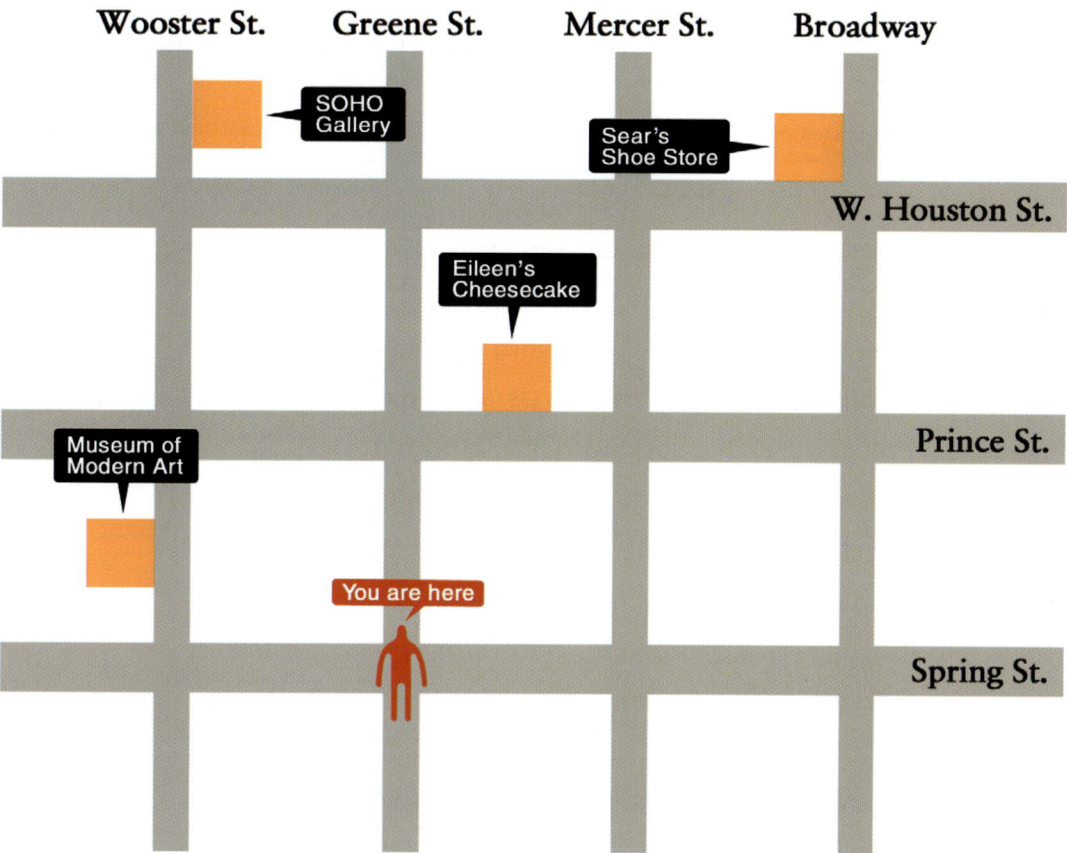

Pronunciation

Read aloud the words below. Then listen to the recording and mark the stress in each word.

> **e.g.** spórts center

1 drugstore
2 shopping mall
3 post office
4 newsstand
5 movie theater

6 ballpark
7 flower shop
8 parking lot
9 grocery store
10 convenience store

Could you tell me how to get there?

Grammar Exercises

Nice to meet you

A Circle the correct answer.

1. My name (is/are) James Brown. I (am/are) 25 years old.
2. Ted (am/is) from New Zealand. Where (is/are) you from?
3. Cindy and Fred (is/are) in a hospital. They (is/are) doctors.
4. My parents (is/are) both teachers. They (is/are) very kind to students.
5. They (am/are) my students. They (am/are) in the 6th grade now.
6. The students (is/are) on summer vacation. They (is/are) very happy.
7. Mark and Anthony (is/are) brothers. They (is/are) both musicians.
8. Pamela (is/are) very talkative, but her sister (is/are) not.
9. Tom and I (is/are) in the same class. We (is/are) best friends.
10. Amy (is/are) very nice, but her sister (is/are) pretty mean.

B Write the missing words from the box.

| Hello | meet | too | name |

1. **A:** Hi. I'm Mark Anthony.
   B: _____, my _____ is Jessica Jones.
   A: Nice to _____ you, Jessica.
   B: Nice to meet you, _____, Anthony.

| Nice | name | from | Where |

2. **A:** What is your _____?
   B: My name is Kelly Davis.
   A: _____ are you from?
   B: I'm _____ Canada. How about you?
   A: I'm from Australia.
   B: _____ to meet you.

UNIT 02 Who is she?

A Match the questions with the correct answers.

1. What's your name? _____
2. Where are you from? _____
3. How old are you? _____
4. What color is your car? _____
5. What's your telephone number? _____
6. How tall is your brother? _____
7. Who is the girl over there? _____
8. When is your birthday? _____
9. Where is she from? _____
10. Who are they? _____
11. How old is your father? _____
12. What's your nationality? _____

a. It's 646-321-1274.
b. I'm from Korea.
c. He is 185cm tall.
d. He is 45 years old.
e. She's from New Zealand.
f. My name is Samantha Jones.
g. I'm Canadian.
h. She is my cousin.
i. I'm 29 years old.
j. It's black.
k. They are my friends.
l. It's November 16th.

B Write about your partner.

1. What is his / her name?
   → _____

2. When is his / her birthday?
   → _____

3. What is his / her hobby?
   → _____

4. Who is his / her favorite movie star?
   → _____

5. Where is his / her hometown?
   → _____

Grammar Exercises 105

UNIT 03 There is a cell phone on the table

A Underline the wrong words and correct them.

1 Is there a pencil and a notebook on the desk?
   → _____

2 There are not much milk in the fridge.
   → _____

3 How many children is there in your family?
   → _____

4 How much days are there in a month?
   → _____

B Find the correct location of each object in the picture. Put the number of the object next to the proper sentence.

① wallet ② paper clips
③ stapler ④ mirror
⑤ shoes   ⑥ clock

1 It's in the drawer.
   → ____

2 They're under the desk.
   → ____

3 They're in front of the stapler.
   → ____

4 It's between the wallet and the mirror.
   → ____

5 It's on the right of the stapler.
   → ____

6 It's on the left of the stapler.
   → ____

UNIT 04 That's mine!

A Write the correct words in the blanks.

1. I have a cell phone.
   → It's _____ cell phone. The cell phone is _____.

2. She has a sports car.
   → It's _____ sports car. The sports car is _____.

3. He has a PDA.
   → It's _____ PDA. The PDA is _____.

4. We have some cookies?
   → They're _____ cookies. The cookies are _____.

5. They have a TV?
   → It's _____ TV. The TV is _____.

6. You have a laptop.
   → It's _____ laptop. The laptop is _____.

B Make the questions. The first one is done for you.

1. **A:** Whose bag is this / that?
   B: It's Cindy's bag.

2. **A:** _____
   B: They are my books.

3. **A:** _____
   B: It's Mr. Jefferson's car.

4. **A:** _____
   B: It's Tom's MP3 player.

5. **A:** _____
   B: It's Jane's evening dress.

What are you doing?

A Complete the sentences with the correct form of the verbs below.

look	set	get	play	learn
take	work	listen	enjoy	do

1 Michelle is _____ a shower. She'll go out soon.
2 Jonathan is _____ the table for dinner. He is helping his wife.
3 Amy is _____ on a term paper. It's a very important assignment.
4 My parents are _____ dressed. They are going to a concert tonight.
5 Jack is _____ to music. He loves every kind of music.
6 Morgan is _____ how to snowboard. He wants to be a good snowboarder.
7 My neighbors are _____ chess. They love games so much.
8 Roger is _____ the laundry. It's all dirty.
9 My sister is _____ her new job. She seems to like it.
10 Paula and Jack are _____ for their shoes. They cannot find them.

B Complete the short dialogues using the words provided.

1 Is Brad reading a magazine? (clean the house)
No, he isn't. He is cleaning the house.

2 Is your son sleeping? (play)
No, _____

3 Is Kevin working out at a gym? (relax at home)
No, _____

4 Are they watching TV? (talk on the phone)
No, _____

5 Are you feeling better today? (feel worse)
No, _____

6 Is your mother writing a letter? (read a newspaper)
No, _____

Does he go to work early?

A Fill in the blanks.

1. I drive a bus. My father drives a taxi.
2. My children come back home around 6 o'clock. My husband _____ back home at 8 o'clock.
3. Tyler _____ the piano. His older brother plays the violin.
4. My sister and I watch movies. My mother _____ soap operas.
5. I drink beer everyday. My wife _____ coffee everyday.
6. Susan _____ home for school. Her parents leave for work.
7. My brother _____ cars. I sell computers.
8. You play basketball. Your sister _____ table tennis.
9. We live in San Francisco. Our son and his wife _____ in New York.
10. They work in a hospital. We _____ in a trading company.

B Write the question.

1. _____
   Yes, we do. We watch movies on the weekend.

2. _____
   No, she doesn't take the subway. She drives to work.

3. _____
   Yes, he does. My brother washes his hair everyday.

4. _____
   No, they don't. My parents don't work on Saturday.

5. _____
   No, I don't. I don't play the guitar.

Grammar Exercises 109

UNIT 07 What does she do?

A Match each job title on the left with the proper sentence on the right.

1. nurse _____
2. mechanic _____
3. hairdresser _____
4. chef _____
5. receptionist _____
6. firefighter _____
7. salesperson _____
8. fashion designer _____
9. police officer _____
10. flight attendant _____

a. I cut and perm people's hair.
b. I put out fires.
c. I take care of patients.
d. I sell products to people.
e. I cook food at a restaurant.
f. I design clothing.
g. I fix cars.
h. I protect people from crime.
i. I answer the phone and type.
j. I serve passengers on an airplane.

B Choose the proper question word for each underlined part and make up the question.

What	When	Where	How
Who	How long	What time	

1. Pamela goes hiking on the weekend. → _____
2. Don takes the subway to work. → _____
3. Jonathan goes to the Best Theater to see a play. → _____
4. Gina gets home from work at 9 p.m. → _____
5. It takes six hours to get to the ski resort. → _____
6. I play tennis with my friends on Sunday morning. → _____
7. Kelly often has a drink at the Bull's with her co-workers. → _____
8. My mother is a history teacher. → _____

Can you dance well?

A Make up questions using the words provided.

1. ride / can / you / a bicycle?
   → _____

2. you / good / video / are / playing / games /at?
   → _____

3. can / do / what / at / you / movie theater / the?
   → _____

4. get / you / how / to / do / school?
   → _____

5. have / Chinese / where / you / food / can / good?
   → _____

B Complete the chart below with your own information and answer the questions using the information in the chart.

	Sports	Languages	Games	Musical instruments
I can...				
I can... only a little				
I am good at...				
I can't...				

1. What are you good at? → _____
2. What can you do? → _____
3. What can't you do? → _____
4. What can you do only a little? → _____
5. What sports can you play? → _____

Grammar Exercises 111

Where was he last night?

A Complete the following dialogues.

1. **A:** It _____ very hot yesterday.
   B: Yeah, it _____, but it's pretty chilly today.

2. **A:** _____ Pam in time for the meeting?
   B: No, she _____. She _____ late for the meeting.

3. **A:** _____ were Anna and Peter this morning?
   B: They _____ at the gym.

4. **A:** _____ your sisters at the movies last night?
   B: No, _____ _____. They _____ at the concert.

5. **A:** _____ was Andy at the gallery?
   B: He _____ there a week ago.

6. **A:** _____ _____ you with at the shopping center?
   B: I _____ _____ my parents.

B Fill in the blanks with the proper words from the box. Use the correct form of each verb.

job	shop	get	ride
watch	look	bowl	eat

1. I was _____ in the park last night.
2. Steve was _____ a jetski at the beach.
3. Sarah and Pete were _____ the parade at the amusement park.
4. Nicole and I were _____ a lot at the restaurant.
5. She was _____ at the mall.
6. They were _____ at the bowling alley.
7. My grandmother was _____ at old paintings at the museum.
8. Cathy was _____ a haircut at the beauty salon.

What did you do yesterday?

A Complete each sentence by putting the correct past form of the verb in the blanks.

1 They _____ (fix) the sink and the bath tub.
2 Mandy _____ (relax) at home and _____ (listen) to music last night.
3 Chris _____ (play) golf with his close friends last weekend.
4 Jason _____ (take) a day off and _____ (go) to the hospital.
5 My friend _____ (invite) me over to dinner yesterday.
6 Linda _____ (talk) to her boss about the plan.
7 Dana _____ (meet) her old friends at the bar.
8 They _____ (order) a stereo through mail order.

B Write questions with *What*, *When*, *Where*, *Who* or *How*.

> **e.g.** I played golf at the Good View Country Club.
> → What did you do?

1 Sally invited her co-workers over to dinner.
   → _____

2 They had a picnic at Riverside Park on Sunday.
   → _____

3 I bought a dress at the department store.
   → _____

4 Gary happened to meet his ex-girlfriend on the street last Friday.
   → _____

5 Robin took the shuttle bus to the airport.
   → _____

6 Mr. Edwards and his employees went hiking in Mt. Colorado.
   → _____

Grammar Exercises   113

How many apples do you need?

A Complete each sentence with the appropriate word.

1 There are many dishes in the cabinet. (many / much)
2 There is _____ money in my wallet. (many / much)
3 I have _____ homework to do tonight. (a / some)
4 She doesn't need _____ drinks. (some / any)
5 There is _____ water in the lake. (few / little)
6 There are _____ oranges in the basket. (a few / a little)
7 He doesn't have _____ brothers or sisters. (some / any)
8 There are _____ ants in this house. (few / little)
9 Some people drink _____ soda. (too many / too much)
10 They cook _____ meatballs. (too many / too much)

B Read each sentence and find the errors. Then correct them.

1 I need a break. Why don't we have a few coffee break?
→ _____

2 He's a gardener, and he owns much flowers.?
→ _____

3 Can you give me an information about the flight to New York?
→ _____

4 How many furniture are there in your apartment?
→ _____

5 We don't have many time before the meeting starts.
→ _____

6 He is hungry, so give him any bread.
→ _____

UNIT 12 I'd like to go rollerblading

A Complete the short dialogues.

1. A: _____ do you like to _____ after work?
   B: I _____ to do some exercises.

2. A: _____ you like _____ _____ DVDs on Sunday?
   B: No, I don't. I like _____ _____ TV.

3. A: Do you want Harry _____ _____ the kitchen?
   B: No, I want _____ to paint the bathroom.

4. A: _____ Brian _____ to go for a drive this afternoon?
   B: Yes, he wants to go to Oak Valley for a drive.

5. A: What _____ David want _____ to do?
   B: He wants me _____ get some bread.

B Put the sentences in order.

1.
   ____ Yes, I am.
   ____ I like to go fishing. How about you?
   __1_ What do you like to do in your free time?
   ____ Oh, are you free this Sunday?
   ____ I like it, too.
   ____ Good. Why not come fishing with my family?

2.
   ____ How much more would you like to have?
   ____ I'd like one more cup.
   ____ Yes, I'd like some.
   __1_ Would you like some more black tea?

3.
   ____ Yes, I am.
   __1_ Would you like to go dancing with me tonight?
   ____ Then are you free tomorrow night?
   ____ Perfect. Can we get together then?
   ____ I'd like to, but I have to go to the dentist.

UNIT 13 He's tall and funny

A Write the questions with *What* or *How*.

1. The umbrella is yellow and green striped.
   → _____

2. The watch is round and the band is red.
   → _____

3. The house is pretty old and huge.
   → _____

4. She is average height and she has black hair.
   → _____

5. He is patient and generous.
   → _____

6. She is wearing a pink sweater and a white skirt.
   → _____

B Answer the two questions using your own information and your partner's information. Write the answers in the space provided.

What are you wearing?

I'm wearing _____
_____
_____
_____

What is your partner wearing?

He / She is wearing _____
_____
_____
_____

UNIT 14 — I go jogging every day

A Put the sentences in the correct order to complete conversations.

1.
   - [ ] Then what do you do?
   - [1] Do you often go to the movies on weekends?
   - [ ] I usually go to concerts.
   - [ ] No, I don't. I rarely go to see a movie.

2.
   - [ ] Yes, she does.
   - [ ] How many times a month does she go bowling?
   - [ ] Every week? She must be a good bowler.
   - [1] Does Linda go bowling a lot?
   - [ ] Almost once a week.

3.
   - [1] What do you like to do in your free time?
   - [ ] Sure.
   - [ ] I like going camping.
   - [ ] At least twice a month.
   - [ ] How often do you go camping?
   - [ ] Twice a month? That's quite often. Can I go with you next time?

B Write your own sentences using the words provided.

| always | usually | often | sometimes | rarely | never |

1. Drink coffee → I rarely drink coffee.
2. Hang out with friends on weekends → _____
3. Go shopping for clothes → _____
4. Stay up late on Saturday night → _____
5. Eat out for dinner → _____
6. Go to a baseball game → _____

What are you going to do tonight?

A Complete each sentence by putting the proper verb with *be going to* in the blank.

| drive | go out | eat out |
| fix | stay up | go gambling |

1. The garage door doesn't work. Tom _____ it.
2. Mrs. Pete doesn't want to cook dinner. Her family _____ tonight.
3. Cecil has a math final exam tomorrow. She _____ late tonight.
4. Samuel feels happy. He _____ for a drink with his wife.
5. Rick and his wife missed the shuttle bus. They _____ to the park.
6. Jeff went to Las Vegas for a vacation. He _____ at casinos.

B Choose the correct expression in the bracket.

1. **A:** I'd like to have some coffee.
   B: (I'll / I'm going to) make some for you.

2. **A:** What would you like to drink?
   B: (I'll / I'm going to) have some tea.

3. **A:** (Will you do / Are you doing) anything this Saturday?
   B: Yes, (I'll go / I'm going) out with my girlfriend.

4. **A:** I don't have any money.
   B: (I'll / I'm going to) lend you some.

5. **A:** Why did you buy flour, butter and sugar?
   B: (I'll / I'm going to) make a cake for my son's birthday party.

6. **A:** When are you getting married?
   B: (I'll get / I'm getting) married next month.

Could you tell me how to get there?

A Amy is new to this city. She wants to go to several places, but she doesn't know the city well. She needs your help.

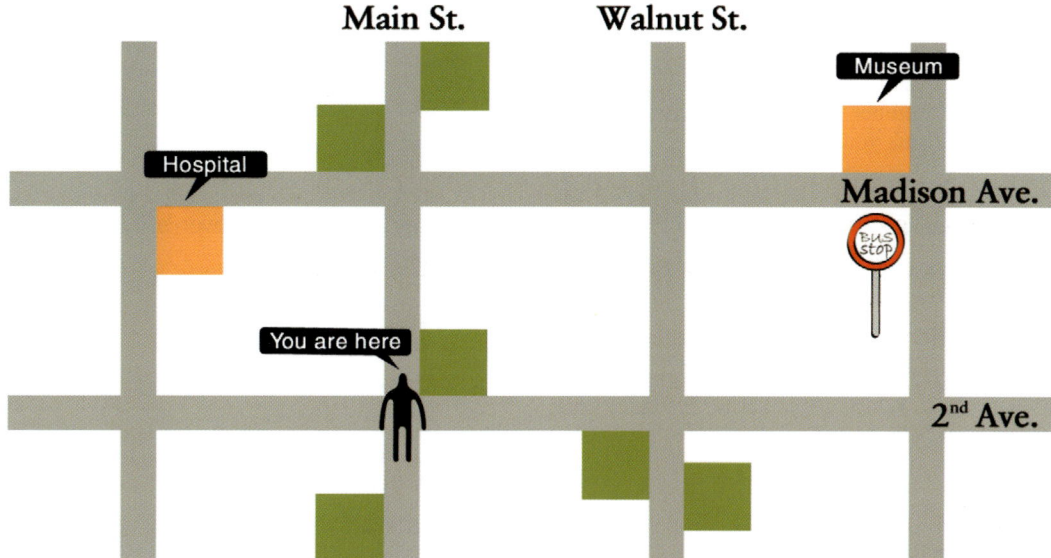

B Complete the dialogues using the expressions in the box below.

| walk up / down | turn left / right | on your left / right |
| go up / down | walk along | across from |

1 Amy: Could you tell me how to get to the bus station?
   You: _____ 2nd Avenue to Walnut Street and turn left. _____ Walnut Street for one block and _____ at Madison Avenue. _____ Madison Avenue and it's _____, _____ the museum.

2 Amy: Do you know how to get to the nearest hospital?
   You: _____ Main Street to Madison Avenue and _____. Then _____ Madison Avenue for one block. It's _____.

3 Amy: How can I get to the museum?
   You: _____ Main Street for one block and _____ on Madison Avenue. Then _____ Madison Avenue for two blocks. It's _____.

Listening Script

Unit 01 Nice to meet you

Listen

Listen to the recordings and complete the table below.

Hi, this is Kevin. I can't answer the phone right now, so please leave your number and I will call you back as soon as possible. Thank you.

1 Hi, Kevin. This is Lisa. Please call me at 505-2700 when you get home.
2 Hey! This is Jon. I need to talk to you. My number is 711-3469. Call me, OK?
3 Hello, Kevin. It's Alice. My cell phone number has changed. It's 010-3216-1274.
4 Hi! It's me, Chris. Where are you now? Please call me at 829-7824, OK?

Unit 02 Who is she?

Listen

Listen to the six sentences. They are the responses to the questions on the left. Match each response with the correct question.

1 Al Pacino is my favorite actor.
2 It is a small car.
3 He is Canadian.
4 It is December 25th.
5 It is at 12:30.
6 It is blue and white.

Unit 03 There is a cell phone on the table

Listen

Listen to the descriptions of the house and check(✓) whether each sentence is correct or incorrect.

1 There is a big mirror in the bedroom.
2 There is a sofa in the living room.
3 There are four chairs in the kitchen.
4 There aren't two bathrooms in this house.
5 There is one coffee table in the living room.
6 There isn't a refrigerator in the kitchen.

Unit 04 That's mine!

Listen

Listen to two people asking and answering questions. Check(✓) **R** if the answer is right. Check(✓) **W** if the answer is wrong.

1 Q: Who is the woman over there?
   A: It is my mother's.
2 Q: Whose books are those?
   A: They are mine.
3 Q: Whose house is that?
   A: It is theirs.
4 Q: What are these?
   A: They are on the table.
5 Q: Are those cats yours?
   A: No, they are Cathy's.
6 Q: Where are your glasses?
   A: They are not mine.
7 Q: Is this Tom's glove?
   A: Yes, it is his glove.
8 Q: Whose cell phone is this?
   A: Yes, it's mine.

Unit 05 What are you doing?

Listen

Listen to each short conversation. Then choose the correct answer to the question.

1 A: Is Sue in the office?
   B: Yes, she is.
   A: Is she working on the computer?
   B: No, she isn't. She is talking on the phone.
2 A: Hey, Ted! Did you have lunch?
   B: I'm having it now.
   A: What are you having?
   B: I'm eating a sandwich.

3 A: Where are Susie and Jacob going? Are they going to the gym?
B: No, they aren't. They're going to the hospital. Their son is in the hospital.

4 A: What's that noise? Is somebody in the kitchen?
B: Maria's in the kitchen.
A: What is she doing there? Is she making tea?
B: No, she isn't. She is making coffee.

Does he go to work early?

Listen

Listen to the conversations and check(✓) if each statement is true or false.

1 A: What does Jason do after work?
B: He usually gets off work early and goes to the gym.
A: Oh, I envy him.

2 A: Does Mary go shopping often?
B: Yes, she does. She goes shopping every weekend.
A: She must be rich!

3 A: Does Brian have his own car?
B: Yes, he does. But he usually walks.
A: Well, walking is good for health.

4 A: What do Mr. and Mrs. Diaz do on the weekend?
B: I think they usually stay home and relax.
A: Don't they go hiking or something?
B: Not that I know of.

07 What does she do?

Listen

Listen to four short conversations and choose the correct answer for each question.

1 A: Does Alice still finish work late these days?
B: No, she doesn't. She's not that busy these days.
A: Then what does she usually do after work?
B: She goes swimming or relaxes at home.
A: Good for her.

2 A: What do Peter and Nancy do on weekends? They look pretty busy on weekends.
B: They take a Japanese class.
A: Oh, right. I heard they're going to travel Japan soon.

3 A: Where does David have lunch?
B: He usually has lunch at the Wendy's near the office.
A: Junk food is not good for his health.
B: I'm worried, too.

4 A: Who does Tony practice dancing with?
B: He practices dancing with his friends from the dancing club.
A: Oh, he does? I want to see him dance someday.
B: Me too.

 Can you dance well?

Listen

Listen to the conversation and check who can do the things in the chart.

A: Who can type fast?
B: Well, **Brenda** types very fast. She can type 500 words a minute.
A: How about driving? Does Clara drive well?
B: No, she can't drive at all. I think **Don** is a good driver.
A: Then can Don dance, too?
B: No, he's not good at dancing. **Patrick** can dance.
A: And how about **Clara**? What can she do well?
B: Well, she is a good baker. Her apple pie is fantastic.

##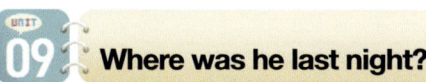

Listen

Listen to the conversations and choose the correct answer to each question.

Conversation 1

A: Was Karen with you at home last night?
B: No, she wasn't.
A: Then who was she with?
B: She was with her boyfriend, Jack.
A: Where were they?
B: They were at Peter's birthday party.

Conversation 2

A: Jason, how was the movie?
B: It was boring.
A: Really? Who were you with at the movie?
B: I was with Michelle.
A: Was she bored too?
B: Yes, she was.

Conversation 3

A: Were you at the gym last night?
B: Yes, I was there.
A: What about Peter? Was he there, too?
B: Uh-huh. He was running on the treadmill.
A: How about you? What were you doing?

Listening Script 121

B: I was lifting weights.
A: Wow. That's a good way to get muscles.

UNIT 10 — What did you do yesterday?

Listen

You will hear a short biography about Tiger Woods. Listen carefully and choose the correct answer for each question.

> Tiger Woods is a successful golfer. He was born in 1975 in California. He started playing golf at the age of two. He went to Stanford University for two years but dropped out to become a professional golfer. He won 12 major professional golf championships and over 53 games on the PGA Tour. He now earns a lot of money every year.

UNIT 11 — How many apples do you need?

Listen

Cathy and Mark had dinner at a fancy restaurant yesterday. Listen to the recording and write **C** for the food that Cathy had and **M** for the food that Mark had.

> Yesterday was Cathy and Mark's 2nd wedding anniversary. They had dinner together at a nice restaurant. Cathy had garden salad and seafood pasta with a glass of pineapple juice. And for the dessert, she ate a piece of apple pie. Mark had a bowl of broccoli soup and New York steak with iced tea. And for the dessert, he ate a chocolate brownie.

UNIT 12 — I'd like to go rollerblading

Listen

Listen to the conversations and check(✓) whether the statements are true or false.

Conversation 1

A: Hey, Greg.
   Do you have any plans for this weekend?
B: No, not yet.
A: Oh, that's good. I'd like to go to the zoo. Would you like to go with me?
B: I'm really sorry, but I'm scared of animals.

Conversation 2

A: Jack, what would you like to do this summer vacation?
B: I'd like to stay in a nice resort near a beach.
A: Sounds fantastic. Where would you like to go?
B: I'm thinking of going to Bali. What about you? Do you have any plans for the vacation?
A: Not yet.

Conversation 3

A: Michelle, are you going to take the day off tomorrow?
B: Yeah, I think I need to get away from work.
A: So, what would you like to do on your day off?
B: I'd like to spend time with my close friends. I haven't seen them for a while.

Conversation 4

A: Mark, I know you like going hiking in the mountains.
B: Yeah, I go hiking almost every weekend. I'm going this Saturday, too. Would you like to go with me?
A: I'd love to, but I have to move to a new apartment.
B: Oh, do you want me to help you? I can go hiking on Sunday instead.
A: Don't worry. I'll be fine. My brothers are coming to help me.

UNIT 13 — He's tall and funny

Listen

Listen to the conversations and circle the answer to each question.

Conversation 1

A: Mom, I can't find my dress.
B: Hmm, what does it look like?
A: Well, it's a blue dress with white polka dots.
B: Does it have a belt in the front?
A: Yes, it does.
B: I saw it in the box under the bed.
A: Oh, thanks mom.

Conversation 2

A: Mark, I heard you bought a new car.
B: Yes, I bought it yesterday.
A: So, tell me about your car.
B: Well, it's a black medium-sized sedan.
A: Does it have four doors?
B: Yes, it does. And there's a sunroof, too.
A: Wow, sounds nice!

Conversation 3

A: Alice, how was the blind date?
B: It was great. I really liked him.

A: That's good. Tell me about him. What's he like?
B: He is kind and smart.
A: And handsome?
B: Yes, he is. He is pretty tall and has blue eyes and dark brown hair.
A: Wow, cool!

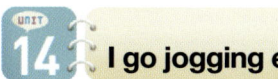

I go jogging every day

Listen

Listen to the four conversations and check the correct box.

Conversation 1

A: Tom, do you know how to play golf?
B: Sure, I like to play it.
A: How often do you play golf?
B: Well, I used to play golf every day, but I'm so busy these days, so I sometimes play it twice or three times a week.
A: Wow, you must be good at playing golf!
B: Pretty much.

Conversation 2

A: Do you know that Julie is an expert at bowling?
B: Oh, really? I didn't know that.
A: She practices a lot.
B: How often does she practice?
A: She always practices; she never misses a day.
B: Wow, she's a very diligent person.

Conversation 3

A: Peter, what are you doing?
B: I'm making a latte.
A: You make lattes yourself?
B: Yes, I love drinking espresso, so I bought this espresso machine.
A: So, how often do you drink espresso?
B: Every day! I can't live without it!
A: I don't think you should drink so much espresso.

Conversation 4

A: Kelly, isn't this the non-smoking section?
B: That's right. I hate the smell of smoke.
A: But I need to smoke!
B: Come on! You should stop smoking. It's bad for your health.
A: I know, but it's really hard. Don't you ever smoke?
B: I never smoke.
A: Okay, okay. Let's just sit here.

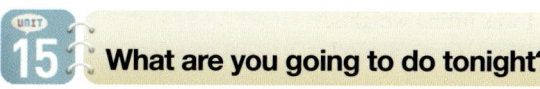

Listen

A. Charles is talking to Michael about the housewarming party at his place. Listen to the conversation and answer the following questions.

Charles: Michael, I'm going to have a housewarming party this Friday. Can you come?
Michael: Oh, sure. I'd love to.
Charles: Great. It will start at 7:00 p.m.
Michael: By the way, what's for dinner?
Charles: We're going to have a barbecue.
Michael: Wow!
Charles: Then I'm going to make some cocktails for the guests.
Michael: Great. I can't wait.
Charles: It'll be fun. See you then.

B. Mandy is talking to Christine about her blind date yesterday. Listen to the conversation and check whether each sentence is true or false.

Christine: Mandy, how did your blind date go?
Mandy: It wasn't bad. He was kind and smart.
Christine: So? Are you going to see him again?
Mandy: Uh-huh, I'll see him again. I want to get to know him more.
Christine: You should. You can never know everything about a person on the first date. So, when will you meet him?
Mandy: Maybe this Saturday. He is going to call me tonight.
Christine: Well, good luck!

 Could you tell me how to get there?

Listen

Where do you want to go in SOHO? Now you are on the corner of Greene Street and Spring Street. Listen to the directions and number the places on the map.

1 Go straight on Greene Street and turn right on Prince. You'll see it on your left.

2 Go one block west on Spring Street and turn right on Wooster. Walk up two blocks and it's on your right.

3 Go two blocks east on Spring. Then walk up two blocks to W. Houston. It's on the corner of Broadway and W. Houston.

4 Go one block to west on Spring and turn right on Wooster. Walk up just a little, and it's on your left.

Listening Script 123

Answer Key for Pronunciation

01 Nice to meet you

Listen to the following words and underline the stressed part in each word.

Ko**re**a   Ko**re**an
Japan   Japa**ne**se
Canada   Ca**na**dian
China   Chi**ne**se
Italy   I**ta**lian
Germany   **Ger**man
France   **French**
Thailand   **Thai**

02 Who is she?

A. Listen to the words and circle the correct ending of each word.

1 seventeen   -teen
2 twenty   -ty
3 forty   -ty
4 fifteen   -teen

B. Listen to the following numbers and choose the correct spelling of each number from the list below.

1 twelfth
2 twenty-first
3 third
4 thirty-second
5 fifty-fifth

03 There is a cell phone on the table

Listen to each word and put it into the appropriate category according to which sound the final 's' makes.

1 newspapers   /s/
2 cameras   /z/
3 clocks   /s/
4 watches   /iz/
5 purses   /iz/
6 keys   /z/
7 stamps   /s/
8 rugs   /z/

04 That's mine!

A. Listen and circle the sentence you hear.

1 Eat your apple.
2 Look at the dogs.
3 Clean the rooms.
4 Pick up the pencil.
5 Did you fill the tanks?
6 Wash the car.
7 Can you see the pictures?
8 Did you meet his sisters?

B. Listen and fill in the blanks.

1 Brad is `my` best friend. I like `his` personality.
2 Jason loves `his` dog. `Its` name is Piggy.
3 Kate and `her` husband like shopping.
4 Maggie's family have `their` own house.
5 You look great. I like `your` hairstyle.

05 What are you doing?

Listen to the questions and check (✓) whether the intonation is rising or falling.

1 What is she having? ↓
2 Are they coming, too? ↓
3 Where are you going? ↑
4 Who's talking to Professor Smith? ↑
5 Is Mark doing his homework? ↑
6 What are Kevin and Brad reading? ↓
7 Are you joking now? ↓
8 Who's making this noise? ↓

Does he go to work early?

Listen to each word and check(✓) the ending sound you hear.

1 dances /iz/
2 studies /z/
3 walks /s/
4 takes /s/
5 goes /z/
6 watches /iz/
7 lives /z/
8 makes /s/

What does she do?

Listen to the questions and complete them by filling in the blanks.

1 (What do you) do on the weekend?
2 (What does he) have for lunch?
3 (Where do you) want to live?
4 (Who does she) play tennis with?
5 (Where do they) stay during the vacation?
6 (What do you) have in your pockets?

Can you dance well?

Listen to the sentences and write either *can* or *can't* in the blanks.

1 Jane can speak a foreign language.
2 Kevin can't play sports well.
3 I can tell you many interesting stories.
4 Marvin and Chris can swim, but they can't dive.
5 My students can't go on a picnic tomorrow.
6 Mr. Heather can drive well at night.

Where was he last night?

Listen to the following sentences and circle the correct words.

1 Max (wasn't) having lunch with his wife.
2 Christina (was) sleeping in her bed.
3 Maria and her husband (were) talking to the doctor.
4 My father (wasn't) enjoying the parade.
5 Last night, my parents (were) shopping at the mall.
6 Michelle (wasn't) enjoying the movie.
7 Many people (were) attending the concert.
8 Yesterday, I (was) playing with my cousin.

What did you do yesterday?

Listen to the following verbs and check(✓) the correct /d/, /t/, or /id/ ending sound.

1 played /d/
2 wanted /id/
3 washed /t/
4 listened /d/
5 needed /id/
6 practiced /t/
7 shopped /t/
8 liked /t/

How many apples do you need?

You will hear one of the words in each of the following pairs. Listen and circle the word you hear.

1 pin
2 fill
3 peel
4 pan
5 leaf
6 strife
7 copy
8 sniff

I'd like to go rollerblading

Listen to the following sentences and fill in the blanks with the words you hear.

1 I want to become a famous physician when I grow up.
2 I'm going to visit my grandmother's house this Saturday.
3 Don't worry. He's going to pay the bill.
4 They want to spend their vacation in Santa Monica this summer.
5 Jennifer loves traveling. She's going to travel around France.
6 Kevin, is this what you want to have?

Answer Key for Pronunciation 125

Unit 13 — He's tall and funny

Listen to the following sentences and fill in the blanks with the words you hear.

1 Would you like some coffee **or** tea?
2 Did you say both pink **and** yellow T-shirts?
3 Will it be cash **or** charge?
4 Is it cheap **and** useful?
5 Do you want diet **or** regular Coke?
6 Do you have a driver's license **or** other identification?
7 I'd like to have fish **and** chips, please.
8 Is it for here **or** to go?

Unit 14 — I go jogging every day

Listen to the following sentences and circle the stressed words.

1 How (often) do you (go) to the (movies)?
2 How many (times) a (week) do you (work) late?
3 She (never) goes (out) for (drinks).
4 (Jasmine) (goes) to the (movies) twice a (week).
5 I saw a (movie) last (night) with my (girlfriend).
6 Can you (help) me with my (homework)?
7 This (watch) (can) (tell) you the (date).
8 (What) does he (look) like?

Unit 15 — What are you going to do tonight?

You will hear one of the words in each of the following pairs. Listen and circle the word you hear.

1 fly
2 river
3 rock
4 light
5 play
6 grass
7 cloud
8 wrong

Unit 16 — Could you tell me how to get there?

Read aloud the words below. Then listen to the recording and mark the stress in each word.

1 drúgstore
2 shópping mall
3 póst office
4 néwsstand
5 móvie theater
6 bállpark
7 flówer shop
8 párking lot
9 grócery store
10 convénience store

Answer Key for Grammar Exercises

01 Nice to meet you

A Circle the correct answer.

1. My name (**is**) James Brown. I (**am**) 25 years old.
2. Ted (**is**) from New Zealand. Where (**are**) you from?
3. Cindy and Fred (**are**) in a hospital. They (**are**) doctors.
4. My parents (**are**) both teachers. They (**are**) very kind to students.
5. They (**are**) my students. They (**are**) in the 6th grade now.
6. The students (**are**) on summer vacation. They (**are**) very happy.
7. Mark and Anthony (**are**) brothers. They (**are**) both musicians.
8. Pamela (**is**) very talkative, but her sister (**is**) not.
9. Tom and I (**are**) in the same class. We (**are**) best friends.
10. Amy (**is**) very nice, but her sister (**is**) pretty mean.

B Write the missing words from the box.

1. A: Hi. I'm Mark Anthony.
   B: **Hello**, my **name** is Jessica Jones.
   A: Nice to **meet** you, Jessica.
   B: Nice to meet you, **too**, Anthony.
2. A: What is your **name**?
   B: My name is Kelly Davis.
   A: **Where** are you from?
   B: I'm **from** Canada. How about you?
   A: I'm from Australia.
   B: **Nice** to meet you.

02 Who is she?

A Match the questions with the correct answers.

1. What's your name? → **f** My name is Samantha Jones.
2. Where are you from? → **b** I'm from Korea.
3. How old are you? → **i** I'm 29 years old.
4. What color is your car? → **j** It's black.
5. What's your telephone number? → **a** It's 646-321-1274.
6. How tall is your brother? → **c** He is 185cm tall.
7. Who is the girl over there? → **h** She is my cousin.
8. When is your birthday? → **l** It's November 16th.
9. Where is she from? → **e** She's from New Zealand.
10. Who are they? → **k** They are my friends.
11. How old is your father? → **d** He is 45 years old.
12. What's your nationality? → **g** I'm Canadian.

B Write about your partner.

1. His / Her name is...
2. It's...
3. His / Her hobbies are...
4. His / Her favorite movie star is...
5. His / Her hometown is...

03 There is a cell phone on the table

A Underline the wrong words and correct them.

1. Is - Are
2. are - is
3. is - are
4. much - many

B Find the correct location of each object in the picture. Put the number of the object next to the proper sentence.

1. **6** clock
2. **5** shoes
3. **2** paper clips
4. **3** stapler
5. **4** mirror
6. **1** wallet

04 That's mine!

A Write the correct words in the blanks.

1. It's **my** cell phone. The cell phone is **mine**.
2. It's **her** sports car. The sports car is **hers**.
3. It's **his** PDA. The PDA is **his**.

4 They're our cookies. The cookies are ours.
5 It's their TV. The TV is theirs.
6 It's your laptop. The laptop is yours.

B Make the questions. The first one is done for you.

2 A: Whose books are these / those?
3 A: Whose car is this / that?
4 A: Whose MP3 player is this / that?
5 A: Whose evening dress is this / that?

UNIT 05 What are you doing?

A Complete the sentences with the correct form of the verbs below.

1 Michelle is taking a shower. She'll go out soon.
2 Jonathan is setting the table for dinner. He is helping his wife.
3 Amy is working on a term paper. It's a very important assignment.
4 My parents are getting dressed. They are going to a concert tonight.
5 Jack is listening to music. He loves every kind of music.
6 Morgan is learning how to snowboard. He wants to be a good snowboarder.
7 My neighbors are playing chess. They love games so much.
8 Roger is doing the laundry. It's all dirty.
9 My sister is enjoying her new job. She seems to like it.
10 Paula and Jack are looking for their shoes. They cannot find them.

B Complete the short dialogues using the words provided.

2 he isn't. He's playing.
3 he isn't. He's relaxing at home.
4 they aren't. They are talking on the phone.
5 I'm not. I'm feeling worse.
6 she isn't. She is reading a newspaper.

UNIT 06 Does he go to work early?

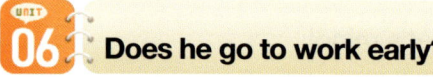

A Fill in the blanks.

2 My children come back home around 6 o'clock. My husband comes back home at 8 o'clock.

3 Tyler plays the piano. His older brother plays the violin.
4 My sister and I watch movies. My mother watches soap operas.
5 I drink beer everyday. My wife drinks coffee everyday.
6 Susan leaves home for school. Her parents leave for work.
7 My brother sells cars. I sell computers.
8 You play basketball. Your sister plays table tennis.
9 We live in San Francisco. Our son and his wife live in New York.
10 They work in a hospital. We work in a trading company.

B Write the question.

1 Do you watch movies on the weekend?
2 Does she take the subway to work?
3 Does your brother wash his hair everyday?
4 Do your parents work on Saturday?
5 Do you play the guitar?

UNIT 07 What does she do?

A Match each job title on the left with the proper sentence on the right.

1 nurse → **c** I take care of patients.
2 mechanic → **g** I fix cars.
3 hairdresser → **a** I cut and perm people's hair.
4 chef → **e** I cook food at a restaurant.
5 receptionist → **i** I answer the phone and type.
6 firefighter → **b** I put out fires.
7 salesperson → **d** I sell products to people.
8 fashion designer → **f** I design clothing.
9 police officer → **h** I protect people from crime.
10 flight attendant → **j** I serve passengers on an airplane.

B Choose the proper question word for each underlined part and make up the question.

1 What does Pamela do on the weekend?
2 How does Don go to work?
3 Where does Jonathan go to see a play?
4 What time does Gina get home from work?
5 How long does it take to get to the ski resort?
6 When do you play tennis with your friends?
7 Who does Kelly often have a drink with at the Bull's?
8 What does your mother do?

UNIT 08 Can you dance well?

A Make up questions using the words provided.

1. Can you ride a bicycle?
2. Are you good at playing video games?
3. What can you do at the movie theater?
4. How do you get to school?
5. Where can you have good Chinese food?

B Complete the chart below with your own information and answer the questions using the information in the chart.

1. I'm good at playing the piano.
2. I can play table tennis.
3. I can't play video games.
4. I can speak French only a little.
5. I can ski.

UNIT 09 Where was he last night?

A Complete the following dialogues.

1. A: It **was** very hot yesterday.
   B: Yeah, it **was**, but it's pretty chilly today.
2. A: **Was** Pam in time for the meeting?
   B: No, she **wasn't**. She **was** late for the meeting.
3. A: **Where** were Anna and Peter this morning?
   B: They **were** at the gym.
4. A: **Were** your sisters at the movies last night?
   B: No, **they** **weren't**. They **were** at the concert.
5. A: **When** was Andy at the gallery?
   B: He **was** there a week ago.
6. A: **Who** **were** you with at the shopping center?
   B: I **was** **with** my parents.

B Fill in the blanks with the proper words from the box. Use the correct form of each verb.

1. I was **jogging** in the park last night.
2. Steve was **riding** a jetski at the beach.
3. Sarah and Pete were **watching** the parade at the amusement park.
4. Nicole and I were **eating** a lot at the restaurant.
5. She was **shopping** at the mall.
6. They were **bowling** at the bowling alley.
7. My grandmother was **looking** at old paintings at the museum.
8. Cathy was **getting** a haircut at the beauty salon.

UNIT 10 What did you do yesterday?

A Complete each sentence by putting the correct past form of the verb in the blanks.

1. They **fixed** the sink and the bath tub.
2. Mandy **relaxed** at home and **listened** to music last night.
3. Chris **played** golf with his close friends last weekend.
4. Jason **took** a day off and **went** to the hospital.
5. My friend **invited** me over to dinner yesterday.
6. Linda **talked** to her boss about the plan.
7. Dana **met** her old friends at the bar.
8. They **ordered** a stereo through mail order.

B Write questions with What, When, Where, Who or How.

1. Who did Sally invite over to dinner?
2. Where did they have a picnic on Sunday?
3. What did you buy at the department store?
4. When did Gary happen to meet his ex-girlfriend on the street?
5. How did Robin go to the airport?
6. Where did Mr. Edwards and his employees go hiking?

UNIT 11 How many apples do you need?

A Complete each sentence with the appropriate word.

2. There is **much** money in my wallet.
3. I have **some** homework to do tonight.
4. She doesn't need **any** drinks.
5. There is **little** water in the lake.
6. There are **a few** oranges in the basket.
7. He doesn't have **any** brothers or sisters.
8. There are **few** ants in this house.
9. Some people drink **too much** soda.
10. They cook **too many** meatballs.

Answer Key for Grammar Exercises 129

B Read each sentence and find the errors. Then correct them.

1. a few - a little
2. much - many
3. an - some
4. many - much   are - is
5. many - much
6. any - some

Unit 12 I'd like to go rollerblading

A Complete the short dialogues.

1. A: **What** do you like to **do** after work?
   B: I **like** to do some exercises.
2. A: **Do** you like **to** **watch** DVDs on Sunday?
   B: No, I don't. I like **to** **watch** TV.
3. A: Do you want Harry **to** **paint** the kitchen?
   B: No, I want **him** to paint the bathroom.
4. A: **Does** Brian **want** to go for a drive this afternoon?
   B: Yes, he wants to go to Oak Valley for a drive.
5. A: What **does** David want **you** to do?
   B: He wants me **to** get some bread.

B Put the sentences in order.

1.
   - 5 Yes, I am.
   - 2 I like to go fishing. How about you?
   - 1 What do you like to do in your free time?
   - 4 Oh, are you free this Sunday?
   - 3 I like it, too.
   - 6 Good. Why not come fishing with my family?
2.
   - 3 How much more would you like to have?
   - 4 I'd like one more cup.
   - 2 Yes, I'd like some.
   - 1 Would you like some more black tea?
3.
   - 4 Yes, I am.
   - 1 Would you like to go dancing with me tonight?
   - 3 Then are you free tomorrow night?
   - 5 Perfect. Can we get together then?
   - 2 I'd like to, but I have to go to the dentist.

Unit 13 He's tall and funny

A Write the questions with *What* or *How*.

1. What does the umbrella look like?
2. What does the watch look like?
3. What does the house look like?
4. What does she look like?
5. What is he like?
6. What is she wearing?

B Answer the two questions using your own information and your partner's information. Write the answers in the space provided.

What are you wearing?

I'm wearing a blue sweater, a purple jacket, and black pants. I'm also wearing a ring and silver earrings.

What is your partner wearing?

She's wearing a red blouse and a navy suit. She is also wearing pink shoes.

Unit 14 I go jogging every day

A Put the sentences in the correct order to complete conversations.

1.
   - 3 Then what do you do?
   - 1 Do you often go to the movies on weekends?
   - 4 I usually go to concerts.
   - 2 No, I don't. I rarely go to see a movie.
2.
   - 2 Yes, she does.
   - 3 How many times a month does she go bowling?
   - 5 Every week? She must be a good bowler.
   - 1 Does Linda go bowling a lot?
   - 4 Almost once a week.
3.
   - 1 What do you like to do in your free time?
   - 6 Sure.
   - 2 I like going camping.
   - 4 At least twice a month.
   - 3 How often do you go camping?

5 Twice a month? That's quite often. Can I go with you next time?

B Write your own sentences using the words provided.

2 I always hang out with friends on weekends.
3 I sometimes go shopping for clothes.
4 I often stay up late on Saturday night.
5 I usually eat out for dinner.
6 I never go to a baseball game.

UNIT 15 What are you going to do tonight?

A Complete each sentence by putting the proper verb with *be going to* in the blank.

1 The garage door doesn't work. Tom is going to fix it.
2 Mrs. Pete doesn't want to cook dinner. Her family is going to eat out tonight.
3 Cecil has a math final exam tomorrow. She is going to stay up late tonight.
4 Samuel feels happy. He is going to go out for a drink with his wife.
5 Rick and his wife missed the shuttle bus. They are going to drive to the park.
6 Jeff went to Las Vegas for a vacation. He is going to go gambling at casinos.

B Choose the correct expression in the bracket.

1 A: I'd like to have some coffee.
   B: I'll make some for you.
2 A: What would you like to drink?
   B: I'll have some tea.
3 A: Are you doing anything this Saturday?
   B: Yes, I'm going out with my girlfriend.
4 A: I don't have any money.
   B: I'll lend you some.
5 A: Why did you buy flour, butter and sugar?
   B: I'm going to make a cake for my son's birthday party.
6 A: When are you getting married?
   B: I'm getting married next month.

UNIT 16 Could you tell me how to get there?

A Amy is new to this city. She wants to go to several places, but she doesn't know the city well. She needs your help.

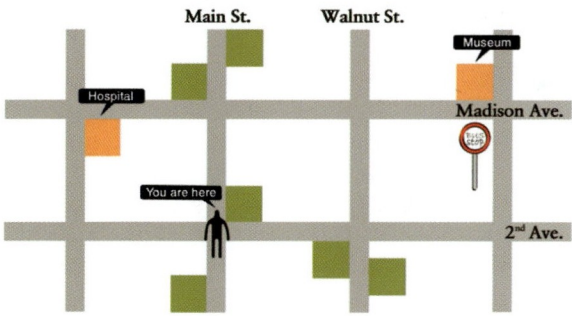

B Complete the dialogues using the expressions in the box below.

1 Amy: Could you tell me how to get to the bus station?

   You: Walk along 2nd Avenue to Walnut Street and turn left.
   Walk up Walnut Street for one block and turn right at Madison Avenue. Walk along Madison Avenue and it's on your right, across from the museum.

2 Amy: Do you know how to get to the nearest hospital?
   You: Walk up Main Street to Madison Avenue and turn left. Then walk along Madison Avenue for one block. It's on your left.

3 Amy: How can I get to the museum?
   You: Go up Main Street for one block and turn right on Madison Avenue. Then walk along Madison Avenue for two blocks. It's on your left.

Answer Key for Grammar Exercises 131

Wanna Talk